THE MOONLIGHT
NIGHTS

THE MOONLIGHT NIGHTS

Uzonna Mabel Anyaoku-Uwalaka

authorHOUSE®

AuthorHouse™
1663 Liberty Drive
Bloomington, IN 47403
www.authorhouse.com
Phone: 1-800-839-8640

Published by AuthorHouse   06/22/2012

ISBN: 978-1-4685-8328-1 (sc)
ISBN: 978-1-4685-8327-4 (e)

To God be the glory.

This book is dedicated to Adiba, Akejinwa, Chukwuemeka Emmanuel, and Henrriata Nwude Anyaoku, who worked very hard in their lives but never lived to enjoy the fruits of their labour. To my late sister, Elizabeth Nwabiachie, and my late brother, Azubike Timothy Anyaoku, who died in their early years.

To my two wonderful sons, Chikezie, Benjamin, Joseph and Ogechukwu, Pius, James Uwalaka, who made my life worth living.

To Tom, Lynne, Margaret, John, and Louise Kyte, who have been pillars of support to me and my children when others have turned their backs on us, even my immediate family. I could never thank them enough for their kindness and support to my son, whom they took into their house, nurtured, and provided for when he returned back to London and had nowhere to go. May God continue to bless them for their kindness and tolerance.

Come rain or come sunshine, Mgbechi was always on the go. Mgbechi was born in a little village called Obosi, very near Onitsha in then Eastern Nigeria, now in Anambara, State of Nigeria. At that time there was no electricity, televisions, or running water in the village. People used to get all their water from the stream, and they entertained themselves with all sorts of activities.

Because there was no electricity, the villagers sometimes used mpanaka, olinma, and kerosene lamps. Some well-off people had what was called gramophones, which were used to play some old records. The gramophones each had a large horn, and the player would be wound until it was full; then the mouth, which had a pin, was then placed on the record and played music like 'Onyeoma Angelina'. Mgbechi felt it was a privilege to have an auntie who had one. Whenever she visited for the weekend, the family enjoyed the music she played with the gramophone. The records were played when everyone had returned from the church, done all the house work and cooking, and had lunch. The music allowed everyone to relax.

During that period the people of the village always looked forward to the moonlight period. The moonlight was very bright, shining like street lamps all over the village playground. It was a night of good omens. At that time there were no cinemas, disco halls, or night clubs. The moonlight period usually lasted between two and four months; it had always been the period everyone in the village was always looking forward to in the future. The moonlight night usually came during the dry season, when the villagers had all harvested their yams, cocoyams, and some other crops. The men had stored all the tubers of yams in the yam barns, and the women had stored their cocoyams in their owokos, a thatched house built with palm leaves. This type of owokos was very cool when one got inside it, and therefore there was always the chance of seeing or touching snakes called eke. The eke is sort of a baby pythons, and they were all over the place because people from the village did not kill them; they believed that the eke protected the ancestors from the evil spirits and did not bite anyone from the village. When they grew bigger, they usually returned to the forest. I thought that after so many years, the ekes would not be around since the then little village has turned into city, but, to my surprise, the ekes are still curling around in the village up until now. Mgbechi could never get use to seeing them around. They were very long, even though people said they were the babies; some of them were as long as eight feet.

The moonlit nights meant a lot to the people in the village then. The young people were always, anxious waiting for the coming of the moonlit night. It was a time of relaxation because all the farm work had been done. There were good and bad things that happened during the moonlit night, but the elders of the village dealt with it all.

During the period, all the able-bodied men and women came out to the Nwobod, the sandy playground where everyone congregated. Each village had its own Nwobod. The Nwobod was kept clean by the villagers, who usually came out every eke day (i.e., every fourth night) to sweep and make sure the ground was covered with sand, to avoid the breaking of legs or arms during play, especially wrestling by the young men. Nwobod was a very important part of the lives of the villagers.

It was at Nwobod, during the moonlit nights, that the village organized many activities. One of the important activities done during that time was the Ima Muo, the masquerade initiation for the young boys between the ages of five and eight years old. Ima Muo gave the boys the right to go out with masquerades during festivals in the village. Any young boy who had not gone through the masquerade initiation was not allowed to go out with masquerades; if he came out to watch or play with masquerades, he would be flogged by masquerades just like the girls. It was a great honour for boys to go through the masquerade initiations.

The preparations to Ima Muo played a very important part in the lives of the young boys. The boys were put into groups, each group being led by some elders and some older boys who had already gone through the initiation. The boys were then taught the rules guiding the masquerade's methodology, the songs, and how to dress up at masquerades. The preparations helped the disciplinary development of the boys, who were taught to respect parents and their elders. They were also taught how to help with house chores and good etiquette. They were meant to understand that if they were bad boys on the day of the initiation, they would receive lots of flogging and be made to carry heavy stones on their heads while crossing a river on a line that would break, making them fall into the river. The young boys were told these things in other to keep them in line.

After one month the boys were then ready to perform the initiation. They would be dressed in the traditional way, with loin cloths.

The girls were also split into groups. Married women and some elders led each group of girls, which had to learn dances that the groups would perform on a set day, when the villagers would choose the group that would represent the village on the inter-tribal dance, held yearly with the neighbouring village. The winning group would receive a huge amount of money. All the girls within the winning group were usually the first group of girls to be picked up by young men for marriage, so every group would do their best to be the winning group.

Mgbechi was in a group with her two of her friends, and she was in the front line. Before a group went out in the middle of the playground to dance, the person in the front would first go out to do the okika. The girls would make themselves up with uhe (a red decoration) and would wear jigidas, with their wrappers and patterns drawn on their bodies and their breasts hanging out. At this point the men would look for the girls with 'ala oba'. Men believed that girls with 'ala oba' never had their breasts droop, even after breastfeeding babies. Those girls were the first to be married. When the girls dressed up with uli, uhe jigida on their heads, hands, necks, and waists they would look great, and the beauty in them would sparkle.

As Mgbechi's group began their dance practice, she was chosen to lead the group. People noticed that Mgbechi was a very good dancer because she was beautiful, tall, and elegant with pointed nipples, which indicated that she had 'ala oba'. Towards the end of the moonlit season, the villagers would then meet together to agree on the night when all the different groups of dancers, both boys and girls, would perform so that the best group would be chosen to represent the village in the inter-tribal festival; other groups like the wrestling team and masquerades would also be chosen. This would be arranged to fall during the next season of moonlight. The groups would be given numbers, and on the competition day they would be called out numerically.

During the moonlit nights, when all the performances would be going, on the elders would lay down very strict rules. Boys must not touch or rape any girl. The punishment for rape was instant castration with no anaesthetic, and then the death penalty. Girls must not lure the boys into committing adultery; the punishment for girls, if found out, was to banish her from the village, never to return again.

In the next moonlight season, the villagers gathered, ready for the competition. The competition started with the girls' dancing groups. As each number was called, the group would start their 'nkwa', their music. The leader of the group would proceed to the centre with a very loud greeting shout, do the okika, and then bow in front of the elders before returning to meet her group, who would by that time be in line waiting for her return. Once the leader joined them the group, they would then dance to the centre.

The numbers continued to be called until it got to the last number group, which was Mgbechi's group. As her group was called, Mgbechi, the leader, came forward, gave a loud greeting, did the okika, and returned to her group, which then moved to the centre. The crowd was ecstatic, shouting, clapping, and screaming. Every eye was on Mgbechi, and in the end her group won the girls' dancing contest.

The last night more people came out to the Nwobod to see what they called mamiwater. Mgbechi's beauty was more than any ordinary person. The young men were more interested in finding the girls that would become their wives.

As Mgbechi's group came to the centre, the ground was about to cave in because many people moved forward trying to get a glimpse of the leader of the group. Some people said that she was a goddess; some said she was mermaid that had come out of the sea, or that she came from another world. Mgbechi danced very well with a beautiful smile on her face. Throughout the dance her teeth glittered like the star. Her group danced so well that it was not difficult to pronounce them as the winning one. The young men could not wait for the girls to leave the centre. Every young man wanted the opportunity to be the first one to speak to Mgbechi, to try to win her heart and make her his wife.

At the end of the girls' competition, it was the boys' turn. The groups were numbered. Each group would decide the type of masquerade that would appear with their group: it could be ulaga, gbogho muo, odogwu anya mee, or more. Each group nominated their own leader. In group one the leader was Okey, group two's leader was Buchi, group three's leader was Emeka, group four's was Chudi, group five's was Maduka, and group six's leader was Ike. Group one performed their dance with its own masquerade, followed by the rest. The girls were already making eyes at the boys of their choice.

When group six was called, the leader, Ike, danced to the centre. What an elegant young man he was—tall, handsome, friendly, and helpful to older people; he fetched water for the widows, helped them do their farm work, helped them fetch firewood for their cooking, and helped them in keeping their compound clean. He was a young man that every mother would wish to have as a son-in-law. When his group emerged to the centre, the crowd screamed, and everyone pushed forward to catch a glimpse of Ike. At the end of the competition, Ike's group came out as the winner.

Mgbechi could not wait to talk to Ike. Ike was fascinated by Mgbechi's beauty and could not wait to meet up with her as well. When Ike and Mgbechi met up with one another, they looked into each other's eyes could see immediate attraction. Ike asked Mgbechi whose daughter she was, where she lived, her surname, who her mother was, and what her mother sold in the market. He also asked Mgbechi what she was doing. Mgbechi told him that she was still attending school, and after school she helped her mother to do some housework and helped father in his farm work. They had a long chat until the end of the night, and with lots of laughter they parted ways.

As Mgbechi was going home, she came across a young girl who was crying and carrying a very heavy bundle of firewood on her head; the bunch was twice her size. Mgbechi stopped her, took the firewood down from her head, and asked for her name, who made her carry such a heavy load, and how far she had been carrying it. The little girl was afraid to stop at first or to answer all her questions, because one older boy was coming behind her. Mgbechi followed her until they reached the house. The little girl looked back and told Mgbechi that she had reached her final destination, but she promised to answer all Mgbechi's questions tomorrow, if

Mgbechi could come by, because her auntie and her son would be going out tomorrow, visiting relatives. When they had gone, she would then have the chance to talk to Mgbechi.

The following day the little girl's auntie and her son went to the nearby village to visit relatives. The little girl made sure that her auntie and her son, who were always keeping watch on her, had really left the house. Then she quickly did all the house chores that were given to her, and she left the house to go and find Mgbechi. As she got close to the udala tree in front of Mgbechi's compound, Mgbechi saw her and came out to meet her. Mgbechi looked at her face and noticed that the little girl was not happy. Mgbechi asked her name and what was making her very sad. Mgbechi also asked her why she was not attending school.

The little girl said in a very faint voice, 'My name is Uzonna.'

'What?' asked Mgbechi.

The little girl again said, 'My name is Uzonna,' this time a bit louder.

Mgbechi said, 'That must be a short form of a longer name.'

The little girl said, 'Yes. My full name is Uzonnasilicho, meaning the way God intended it to be, or the will of God.'

Mgbechi told her that it was a lovely, meaningful name, and she asked her if she knew why her parents gave her such name, because Mgbechi did not know Uzonna's background. Uzonna told Mgbechi that she was unhappy because she had not eaten any food for the past three days—no one had given her any food after all the housework she had been made to do every day. Mgbechi was very sad that such a little girl should be treated in that manner. She asked Uzonna what she had done that made her mother not feed her.

Uzonna started to cry and said, 'She is not my mother.'

Mgbechi told her to stop crying, took her into her house, and asked her mother to please give Uzonna some food to eat. Mgbechi's mother gave some food and water to

Uzonna, and they noticed the speed Uzonna ate all the food, as if there would be none tomorrow. After eating the food and drinking the water, Uzonna knelt down and thanked Mgbechi's mother and Mgbechi, and a smile appeared on her face once more.

Mgbechi then asked Uzonna where her parents were, where was their village, and why was she living with an auntie who was not feeding her. The little girl mumbled some sound, and then tears rolled down her little face. Mgbechi placed her hand on her shoulder and asked her why she was crying. Uzonna told Mgbechi that she had no mother or father—she did not know her mother, had never met her or even seen her photograph. Uzonna said that she could not even imagine what her mother looked like. Uzonna's auntie had always called her a witch. 'My auntie always said that my twin sister and I were witches, because we killed our mother, who died giving birth to us.'

Mgbechi asked Uzonna why her auntie did not feed her. Uzonna said that her auntie always left her without food; she was only given food whenever her auntie's children had leftovers; if they finished their food at each meal, she had to wait until the next one. Sometimes it took days for the children to have some food left over, and in that case Uzonna had to go for several days without food. Uzonna said that sometimes when she was very hungry, she would sneak out of the house pretending to go for firewood, and then would be beg for money to buy something to eat. Sometimes she would be lucky to meet some kind people who would give her some money. 'Sometimes I would go somewhere far from my auntie's house and beg for food, because I would not want to see those who knew my auntie in case they would tell her. If she ever found out, I would receive a thorough beating from her. She would say that I was showing her off to the public, letting them that she had not been feeding me. My auntie likes to appear to people as a very good and kind woman.'

Mgbechi asked Uzonna of my twin sister. She said that she was given to another family and that she had not seen her or heard from her for a very long time. However, her uncle always said that she was alive and well. It was time for Uzonna to go home so as not to be missed at home by her auntie or her children, because that would be big trouble.

Uzonna was not allowed to join the other children to come out for the moonlit play. Mgbechi told her to take heart and said that whenever she was hungry, she should come to Mgbechi's house, and she would give me something to eat. She also told her mother to welcome Uzonna to their house, even if she was not at home. Mgbechi was very concerned about the girl's situation; she even told her mother the story and asked her mother if she knew Uzonna's mother well. At first they did not realise that she was the daughter of the late Adiba, a very kind and helpful woman whom almost all the women in the village liked. Mgbechi's mother said that the day Uzonna's mother died, the village was so quiet and cold; people were shocked that there were cries from everywhere. There was great lamentation that the village had lost one of its most beautiful and kindest women. Mgbechi's mother said that she never knew that the twins survived after the death of their mother. This made Mgbechi more determined to help Uzonna find a way to bring Uzonna out of her auntie's house, where she was going through so much physical abuse, from her auntie and from her auntie's children, who used to kick her about whenever they felt like it. Mgbechi continued to help Uzonna as much as she could. Mgbechi could not do more, because she too was young and was attending school.

The anticipated day for the inter-tribal dancing competition arrived. All dancers from the neighbouring villages came to the Nwobod. Elders from all the different villages and Mgbechi's dancing group also joined the crowd. It was a very big, yearly event that attracted people from other towns, and it was a way of bringing money into the village; it was their tourism for the year, and it was a big opportunity for young ones to get life partners.

As the big day approached, the villagers came out in
to clean up the Nwobod and the village squares, readyi.
the event. After the day's hard work, people went home .o
roast green plantains mixed with ugba, green fresh pepper,
and fresh palm oil, which they would eat before going to
bed.

The following day the villages came out to make apartments
for all the dancing groups from the different towns and
villages. Each apartment was labelled with the name of
the group and town it was allocated to—Nkpor, umoji,
Oba, Obosi, Ogidi, Onitsha, and more—and as each town
arrived, they would be shown their apartment. Before that
the villagers picked some young men and girls who would
be in charge of entertaining the guests, making sure that
they were well looked after. The dance competition would
start the following morning and would go on until the next
morning.

The dance started, and each town got ready, waiting for
their turn. The towns were called alphabetically. The
first town came to the dance floor, and the group danced
very well, followed by the next group. When Mgbechi's
group was called, the group came to the centre, and the
congregation went mad and applauded; the whole area was
shaken. Everyone was taken aback by the beauty dazzling
their eyes, and they wanted Mgbechi.

Mgbechi, who was the group leader, danced like something from the sky. She danced so well and so elegant that was one of the most beautiful girls in the village. All the men that came to Nwobod wished Mgbechi to be their future wife, so they all tried to woo her.

It was then the men's turn, and all the groups were getting ready, also being called alphabetically. The girls were busy choosing their future husbands. Ike's group had its turn. He was very tall and well built, had brown hair, and danced very well. His voice thundered like that of heavy thunderstorm. Mgbechi fell in love with him immediately, and she could barely wait for the group to finish its display. She was already thinking of how and when to see Ike and talk with him.

Mgbechi went to a corner of the playground to see if she could see Uzonna, because she had seen the auntie and her children in the front row on the playground, watching all the events. Unfortunately she did not see Uzonna. As she turned round to return to the main area of the playground she saw Ike coming towards her. She became very excited and a bit nervous. Ike said hello and asked how she was. Mgbechi replied fine and then said, 'You are the most wonderful and best dancer of all the men.' They chatted, and in the end Ike asked Mgbechi to be his wife, and she agreed.

Ike and his family performed all the necessary marriage rights, the traditional marriage was done, the dowry paid, and the arrangements were made for the church wedding. When the wedding was done, the young couple moved to the city, where both of them had a good education and good jobs, and they started their family.

When Mgbechi had her second son, she said that it would be an opportunity to go to the village to inquire if little Uzonna was still living in the village with her auntie. If so, she would ask the auntie if she could take Uzonna to live with her in the city. Mgbechi discussed this with her husband, and they both agreed to the plan.

On the weekend Mgbechi travelled to the village. Her mother was very happy to see her. After she has been welcomed and asked after everybody she knew in the village, Mgbechi told her mother why she had come to the village: she wanted to take Uzonna to the city to live with her, help her with the care of her two sons, and also attend school instead of slaving away in the village for her auntie. Her mother said that it was a very good idea, and it would give the little girl a chance to have a better life. Mgbechi's mother told her she should take good care of Uzonna.

The next day Mgbechi and her mother went to see Uzonna's auntie.

On their way to the house, they saw Uzonna coming back to the house carrying a heavy bunch of firewood on her head. She had no clothes on and no shoes; she looked very tired and had clearly lost some more weight. Mgbechi called to her, and Uzonna was very happy to see Mgbechi and her mother. They offered her a loaf of bread, but as they were very close to Uzonna's house, they could see her auntie standing by the door. Uzonna was afraid to accept the loaf of bread, but her auntie told her to take it. Uzonna's auntie welcomed their visitors, telling them to come in.

Mgbechi and her mother told Uzonna's auntie what they had come to ask. Uzonna's auntie, who had been waiting for an opportunity to get rid of the girl, was delighted at the suggestion of Mgbechi taking Uzonna to the city with her. Uzonna's auntie was not interested in the goodwill of Uzonna but was more interested in what she would get from Mgbechi and her mother. The thought of Uzonna travelling to the city with Mgbechi meant a lot of money and goodies for her. She did not ask what Uzonna was going to the city to do—such as whether she would be attending school. All she wanted and asked for was how much money Mgbechi was going to pay her now and monthly.

Mgbechi could notice the lack of love and care towards Uzonna from her auntie. She did not say much but offered the auntie some money and told her that she would be sending her things and money from time to time. Uzonna's auntie was pleased to get rid of her. She went into the house, packed a little bag for Uzonna, gave it to Mgbechi, and said goodbye to Uzonna. Mgbechi was originally going to go home with her mother and return the following day to take Uzonna, but since the auntie had packed Uzonna's belongings, they might as well take her straight away. One could not imagine the happiness Uzonna felt, to leave her auntie's house and go home with Mgbechi. She did not mind if she stayed in the village with Mgbechi or went to the city; the main thing was that she left the unhappy home where she was treated like a slave.

After seeing the state of Uzonna, Mgbechi made up her mind to take care of this little girl, praying that the Lord would help her to make something good of this girl. Uzonna's auntie asked her if she would like to go to the city and live with Mgbechi. Uzonna said yes, and her face became brighter; Mgbechi could see the happiness on her face. Her auntie told her that the city was full of strange people and that she was going to miss her friends in the village. Uzonna was not even thinking about what her auntie was saying; rather she was thinking of how she would be well fed, have clothes and shoes, would not go to the stream to fetch water or to the bush to fetch firewood, and would not receive heavy beatings. But most of all, she would be able to attend school!

Mgbechi's mother and Uzonna's auntie came to an arrangement. Uzonna's auntie tried very hard to make

Mgbechi's mother believe that she was taking good care of Uzonna, but what she was doing was to try to make as much profit as she could. Mgbechi, her mother, and Uzonna left the house and headed to Mgbechi's mother's house, and that was the last time Uzonna's auntie would see her for a very long time. After all was said and done, it was time Uzonna's freedom and the beginning of new life for her. Hence the story of Uzonna began.

Uzonna was one of twin girls; their mother died when they were babies, and she did not know her mother, and had never seen a photograph of her. All she knew was that her mother had seven children, out of whom two died, leaving five of them alive. She also knew what people in the village said about her mother: how tall, elegant, kind, and beautiful she was, and how very hard working. People did say that her father did not deserve her mother. When Uzonna did appear after many years, villagers did not associate her with Adiba, her mother. Once she told a woman that she was Adiba's daughter, and the woman did not believe her, but after she asked Uzonna the names of her brothers and sisters, and Uzonna told her, she reluctantly agreed. Still, she said, 'My God, you are very ugly and short. You do not look anything like your mother; you must have got your ugliness from your father, because you do not look like anybody from Adiba's family.'

The following day, very early in the morning, Mgbechi and Uzonna left the village to travel to the city of Lagos. It was one of the biggest excitements for Uzonna, who had never left the village to travel to anywhere. She got to see a large number of people on the bus. She was lucky to get to sit by the window so, she was very busy watching the cars, the buses, and the people hustling with their items, trying to sell them to passengers any time the buses and cars stopped at the traffic lights. Uzonna was imaging herself carrying some items and crossing the big busy roads. She wondered whether she would be able to speak the broken English that she heard all the people speaking to one another, because in the city there were a lot of people from different parts of the country whose language was not Ibo. Mgbechi, who had now became Uzonna's new auntie, told her that Lagos was a big city, and one had to be extremely careful on the roads and towards the people she met and talked to.

After a long eight hours on the road, they got to Lagos. At the bus garage, Mgbechi's husband, Ike, was waiting to pick them up with their two sons in the car. On seeing their mother, the children ran out of the car to welcome them. Ike remembered little Uzonna from the village. After getting their belongings from the bus, they headed home to Mgbechi's house. Upon reaching home, Mgbechi told Uzonna to freshen up, and she showed her where to keep her little bag containing her belongings. Mgbechi gave her some food to eat. Uzonna was surprised because she knew that Mgbechi had not had time to cook, so asked how the food came about. Mgbechi told her that her husband had cooked all the food for them to eat when they returned from the village. It was such a big thing for Uzonna because she did not know that men cooked—she had never seen her auntie's husband going into the kitchen, let alone cook the food. Uzonna asked Mgbechi if men really did cook and do some housework as well. Mgbechi told her that they did, especially in the city, because men and women went out to work and earned money; it was not like the village, where women always went to the farm, came home, and did all the cooking and housework, waiting on the men.

Uzonna had been thought that men and boys did not cook or do housework because it had always been the duty of women; men only entered the kitchen to take things. That was a lesson to learn and to get used to. Mgbechi then called her children so that they could eat. Uzonna went to get the cups and cutlery, so as to set the table for Mgbechi's children. The children came out, went straight to get the plates and table mats, brought some water, and told Uzonna to put the cups down on the table. Then Mgbechi went to the kitchen, dished out the food, and called her two sons and Uzonna to come to the kitchen to carry their food. Mgbechi told her children that from that day onwards, they would be eating with Uzonna, and they should be nice and respectful to Uzonna, treating her as one of the family. Uzonna was taller and older than them, so they asked their mother if she was their older sister who had been living in the village. Mgbechi said that they should treat her as if she was their sister. Uzonna thought that she was dreaming and wished that the dream should not stop; she could not believe that any family would treat her so kindly.

They had their food, and Uzonna was a bit shy because she had never eaten on a table with people before; she was used to eating on the floor in the kitchen, after her auntie and the children had finished their own food, and then she would start with their leftovers. Uzonna had the tastiest food in her life, and for the first time she had a full belly. It was like a dream, and she wished she would continue to sleep so as not to come out of it. But this was reality that was beginning to unfold.

After they had all eaten and cleared the table, Mgbechi's children went to their room to play. When they noticed that Uzonna was not with them, they came out to call her. Uzonna hesitated, but they told her to go with them. Uzonna joined Okechi and Kelechi in their room, and the three of them played very well together. Uzonna told them some village stories and sang for them. The boys enjoyed it very much, and they then really liked Uzonna. The boys liked the story and the song about good children They wanted Uzonna to teach them the song 'Onye bu ezi nwa' ('Who Is a Good Child). They preferred it to 'Onyebuchi', because when she sang 'Onye bu ezi nwa,' she would say 'obu Okechi' or 'obu Kelechi'. They liked being called good children. The children told their parents of the songs Uzonna had been singing to them, and how she told them that she really loved them so much and that they were good children. Their mother's action, bringing her to live with them, was God's blessing to her. Okechi and Kelechi became very close to Uzonna, and they truly were like two brothers and a sister.

The next morning, after Mgbechi had taken Okechi and Kelechi to school, on her way back she stopped at the market and bought some clothes: underpants, a pair of sandals, and one pair of rubber slip-on shoes for Uzonna, who had no shoes at all. When Mgbechi got home, she called Uzonna and handed her the bag. Uzonna thought that she was meant to take the bag to the bedroom for her madam, so she turned round to walk towards the bedroom. Mgbechi told her, 'The contents of the bag are for you.'

Uzonna was confused. She opened the bag, looked into it, and asked, 'Mummy, did you say that all these are for me?' Mgbechi said yes. Uzonna could not believe this and was stunned; tears rolled down her face. Mgbechi was surprised and asked her if she did not like the clothes. Uzonna was still crying but replied that she liked all the things very much, and she ran to Mgbechi, knelt down in front of her, and said, 'Thank you, thank you! I am so happy! No one has ever bought me new clothes, shoes, and pants. I have always had to take the clothes rejected by my auntie's children. The only dress I had was the one my auntie's daughter gave to me, and that was what I had when you came to take me. I have never had shoes before! May the Lord bless you, Mummy. I promise that I will be a good girl and will always do any job you want me to do in the house.'

Uzonna could not wait for Okechi and Kelechi to come back from school so that she could show them her new clothes and shoes. She was very happy and excited. Mgbechi asked if she would like to attend the same school as Okechi and Kelechi, and Uzonna said with her eyes wide with excitement that she would be very happy to do so. Mgbechi, whom Uzonna now called Mama just like her two sons, told her that tomorrow morning she should wake up earlier, bathe herself, and put on one of the new dresses and her new shoes, so that she could go with her the boys to their school in the morning. It was a great new life for Uzonna. She went with them to the school in the morning, and she looked at the school in amazement as children ran into the school, some going into their classes. She was happy that she was one of them.

When Uzonna returned home with Mama, she took off her new clothes and shoes and went to the kitchen to help Mama with lunch preparation. She heard a noise, looked out, and saw Okechi, Kelechi and their father, Ike. She ran to them, welcomed them, and took the bags from their father. Uzonna asked them how school was, and as soon as they went into the house, Uzonna could not wait to show them all her new clothes and shoes, and also the new school uniform Mama had bought for her. She brought her bag and took out everything, showing them all the things Mama had bought for her. Then she ran to their father, knelt down, and held his feet, saying, 'Thank you, Papa, thank you so much for all the shoes and clothes Mama bought for me! May the good Lord bless you double!'

Papa told her to get up and told her that all he wanted was for to be a good girl at home and at school. They all had their lunch. Okechi and Kelechi did their homework, had a rest, and then went into the sitting room and watched television. Uzonna was very happy to be allowed to sit in the sitting room and watch television with the rest of the family—that never happened when she was living with her auntie. When they were about to go to bed, Mama told Uzonna that she would be going to school with Okechi and Kelechi the next day.

Uzonna could not believe the changes that were coming into her life. Within a very short time, she had joined this family. The first time she had watched television and saw Ukaonu's Club, she enjoyed it very much. All children liked Ukaonu's Club because there was always lots of dancing, both modern and old, and most children learned their dancing from watching the programme. Life had become very good for Uzonna.

They all went to bed to get enough sleep for school the next day. Then Mgbechi reminded Uzonna that she needed to be up early in the morning so as to be ready for school in good time. Because it was her first day at school, she must be early to create a good impression.

The next morning, Okechi, Kelechi, and Uzonna woke up very early, did their usual morning chores, attended to their personal hygiene, and put on their school uniforms. Uzonna put on her new school uniform and sandals. They all had their breakfast and then were off to school. Upon getting to school, Okechi and Kelechi went into their classrooms.

Mgbechi took Uzonna with her, and they went into the headmistress's office. Mgbechi said, 'Good morning, Mrs Azu.'

The headmistress turned around and said good morning and asked how she could be of help. Mgbechi said that she had brought her niece, Uzonna, and she would be very glad if Mrs Azu could admit her into her school. The headmistress replied that she would admit Uzonna because there still vacancy in the school.

The headmistress asked Uzonna which class she thought she could cope with. Mgbechi told the headmistress that it would be better if Uzonna joined the beginners class, because she had never attended any school before. The headmistress took them to the appropriate classroom and introduced them to the class teacher, Mrs Odu. The class teacher welcomed Uzonna, showed her where to sit, and then brought the list of the class requirements and gave it Mgbechi, who thanked her and told her that she would try to provide the things in the list. Then Mgbechi left Uzonna with the other children in the class and went home.

The teacher then asked the class to welcome Uzonna, and introductions were carried out around the class. It was a great for Uzonna: she was happy being in school, and she made friends with all the children. School became a very important part of her life, and she never wanted to miss a day.

The Anene family took great care of Uzonna. With proper feeding, love, and a happy environment, Uzonna blossomed. She enjoyed school and developed a very good relationship with Okechi and Kelechi; they were like brothers and sister, and that was how everybody saw them except for those who knew Mgbechi very well. Things were very positive for Uzonna.

When Uzonna finished her primary school, she was encouraged to sit for an entrance examination into secondary school. Mgbechi gave Uzonna some money to purchase the application forms and paid for her registration for three secondary schools. She completed the forms, submitted them, and then sat for the examinations, passing into two schools. Out of the two she chose one, but her problem was how to get the school fees. Uzonna was still leaving with Mgbechi and her family, enjoying her holiday and not worried much about money.

As the term was drawing near, Mgbechi learnt that her older brother, who was studying abroad, had returned to Nigeria. Her brother, who had studied engineering at Oxford University in London, was employed by the Nigerian

Transport Division to head the Inland waterways. He had a highly paid job, and he agreed to pay Uzonna's school fees at the secondary school.

However, that was to become a very difficult period for Uzonna. She was no longer living with Mr and Mrs Anene, and she missed Okechi and Kelechi, who were at other secondary schools. She had a very miserable time as a student, and her brother did not give her any pocket money; all he did was send her school fees straight to the school, with no extra money for her upkeep. One would have thought that Uzonna's brother would have cared for her well, but it was not so. It was a nightmare, like she had gone back to living with her wicked auntie.

During holidays or half-term breaks, Uzonna would not have money to travel home with her school belongings; she would beg some of her friends to help. Some of her friends, whose parents would come to pick them from school, would kindly give her a lift to the nearest point, where she would be able to walk home. She usually walked home to stay with her stepmother, who could barely feed herself, let alone Uzonna. It was a period of great anxiety because no one knew what was going to happen. Many of the school children were at home, and many returned from the northern part of Nigeria where they were being massacred by the Moslems. In other to try and save some children, all schools were closed.

Many parents were very worried, not knowing what would be the fate of their children. Many children were raped and slaughtered, and most parents could not sleep or eat while they waited to see their children return home. Those who were at the universities and secondary schools were the targets of horrible men who had been angry that Southern girls were allowed to go to school. Most of them made their ways to the residence halls and rounded up girls, raping and killing many of them. As time went on, all the surviving students and parents returned to the South, most of them with nothing. Things were not getting better, and all schools in the southern part of the country were closed down, their students told to go home. Everyone thought that it was a matter of days or weeks before things would return to normal, and all schools would be opened, but that was not the case.

Uzonna had to return home. At home was her twin sister and her brother, all staying with their stepmother. With no money coming from anywhere to run the house, the children had to think of how to survive. They took up farming with their stepmother, planting all sorts of crops: cassava, cocoyam, corn, egusi, ugu, and some ground nuts. The nuts grew within a very short period and had to be harvested on time. Uzonna and her sister, brother, and stepmother harvested the ground nuts and filled up at least three basins. They boiled some, fried some, and took them to the market to sell; some were kept by the side road in front of their house for passers-by to buy. The money from the sale of the ground nuts was used to buy whatever food they could not grow.

Uzonna, her sister, and her brother made lots of friends in the village; most of them were also students. Their stay in the village afforded them the opportunity to know the village, and it also gave them the chance to be together at home, which they never had because they were separated after the death of their mother. Life in the village was very difficult, but knowing that other children were going through the same hardship helped. The well-to-do families had already taken their children out of the country, sending them to other countries where they continued with their education. Children from poorer families were left to fight for their survival. People were confused and did not know what was going on.

The school closure went from weeks to months. News of people returning from the Northern part of Nigeria without their belongings continued. There was also news of people being killed by the Northerners, and houses, shops, and businesses owned by the Ibos were burnt down. The rampage continued, and the government tried to control the disturbances, but to no avail. The anger was directed to the Ibos.

After six months, with no solution found to stop the disturbance, Uzonna and her family heard on the radio that the Easterners had formed a government and had declared an independent state of Biafra, because they felt that the Ibos were not wanted as part of Nigeria. Biafra wanted to exist as it did before the amalgamation of different states by the colonial masters in 1914. Before the amalgamation, there were three states, or clans as they were called at the time: one in the north, one in the west, and the other in the east. Due to the greed of the British government, they joined all the clans together to make it easier for their financial control. After Nigeria gained independence in 1960, the country had never been at peace.

It had not been possible for the Northern Moslems to tolerate the Christians from the South; there had always been hatred for the Christians, especially for the Ibos, whom they found to be very educated, hard working, and also very proud people—hence the killings and the destruction of properties belonging to the Ibos in the North, which was still going on today. When the Easterners called themselves Biafra and wanted to become a country of their own, the British advised the Northern part of the country to allow Biafra to exist as another country, because all the wealth that was in Nigeria was mainly located within Biafra. Nigeria decided to wage war against Biafra. The Northern part of Nigeria had a larger population and larger land mass, and it was supported by the British, who found it very easy to manipulate the Northerners, sapping the oil from Nigeria. The British did not want Biafra to exist independently because people from Biafra were very educated and would not be manipulated by the British. At the time Nigeria was also the world's largest producer of palm oil and palm kernels, and the British people government did not want to lose this resource; hence the Nigeria-Biafra war started and lasted for three years.

There were rallies at market squares for all people, both young and old. Lots of talks were carried out by top Biafran people, telling the crowd why they should be Biafra, the advantages being security and how Biafra would become one of the most beautiful countries in the world. Many young people joined the Biafra army. The morale of the Ibos were at the highest level. The younger ones were trained as militia.

The first year of the war was not bad because the Biafra was doing fine, there was no shortage of food, and people were not dying, though one or two soldiers would lose their lives. Biafra was standing firm against the Nigerian army, which gave everyone courage; most people thought the war was coming to an end.

All of a sudden things began to turn against the Biafran soldiers. People were told that the British government had decided to supply the Nigerian army with ammunition in return for oil. As the British began to supply Nigeria with heavy arms, the Nigerian soldiers started to push the Biafran soldiers back. The British government supplied the Nigerians with fighters, bombers, and tanks, so the army became stronger. There were also some disgruntled soldiers within the Biafran army, and some of them were then bribed by the Nigerian army, so they agreed to sabotage the Biafran army and divulged all the Biafran plans to them, telling them the positions and movements of the army.

The Biafran army suffered heavy losses at a town called Ore. This town was supposed to be the last place where Biafra was to take over, and then the war would come to an end. Due to sabotage, Biafran soldiers were pushed back with heavy loss of lives, and from then on the Biafran soldiers continued to retreat with heavy casualties and lost all the towns they had captured at the beginning of the war. The war, which Uzonna and her new family mostly only heard about on radios, came to their village. The hardships they experienced before was nothing to be compared to what would happen to Uzonna in the future.

It was a beautiful morning, and Uzonna woke up as usual with no particular plan for the day; everyone took life one day at a time, not knowing what would happen the next minute. The main problem for the day was always what to eat. She went to the bushes to try to gather some firewood, and then she returned, checked the melon seeds they had put out under the sun to dry, collected the seeds, and started to peel off the skins. This activity lasted throughout the afternoon, because it was very difficult to peel enough to make a pot of soup. By the time the evening came, she had peeled enough to make a soup. Uzonna had to grind the egusi, pepper, and crayfish on the grinding stone beside the kitchen.

Uzonna ground all the necessary ingredients needed for the soup. As she was grinding things, and her stepmother was cutting the ugu needed for the soup, there was a loud bang on top of the house. The roof caved in, followed by another bang. Everyone ran outside the compound and saw a large number of the villagers running and shouting to take cover. Everybody went flat on the ground as they were taught during training. They were then told that the Nigerian soldiers were dropping shells on the village as they approached. Uzonna was very frightened because whenever the Nigerian soldiers entered a town or village, all the women were raped, and the men and children were killed. Everyone ran out of the village, not looking back, and they didn't stop until they couldn't hear the sound of the shells and bullets.

It took them two days to get to a town where the noise totally disappeared. They noticed then that they all ran out with nothing—they only had whatever they wore at the time they ran out of the house. After they had some rest, it was then that they felt very hungry and thirsty, and then they discovered that when one was running for dear life, one did not feel hungry or thirsty, instead concentrating on getting to a safe place. Hunger was a thing of the mind.

The first thing that came to Uzonna's mind as they were now safe was to look for any members of her family. She went from one camp to another but was not able to any relatives, so she joined the other children at the camp. She felt very lost and lonely, but she felt a bit safe knowing that they were in a church compound with reverend fathers and sisters, and also they were sure of at least one good meal a day. The fathers and sisters were very kind and put the children into small groups of ten. The kids were given some cooked cornmeal with corned beef, with clean drinking water for a change. The relief and happiness on their faces, bodies, and souls were obvious, after starving for many days. Throughout the journey running from the village, they were just plucking any fruits they saw on trees, eating them without washing. Uzonna knew then that most fruits were not dangerous, though some of them gave her an aching stomach. God was looking after them. It would have been a disaster for someone to be ill because there were no doctors on the road, and even if there were, there was no medication to use.

After the children ate, the reverend fathers and sisters came out with some jute bags, opened them, and shared some clothes. They also gave some toilet soaps and told them to go down to the stream and have baths, washing the dirty clothes they had been wearing for weeks. The kids were also given some containers to carry, in order to fetch some water for use in the house, That was how they spent the first week, making sure the compound was kept clean.

One day when they were going down to the stream to fetch water, Uzonna saw a familiar face and ran to her. They embraced each other, and the woman asked Uzonna if she had seen one of her brothers, who was with her family. She answered no and then the woman told her where they were staying and directed her how to get to that particular camp. It was a journey of two days, but half of the way was done on a bicycle because she had money to pay for bicycle transport.

This little money she used to pay for half of the journey was given to her by Sister Mary during one of the masses, which they usually had three times a day. Uzonna summoned up courage, went to Sister Mary, and told her that she had found out where one of her brothers, his wife, and his two sisters-in-law were staying. Uzonna would be happy to go and join them, but her problem was that she had no money to pay for transport. Sister Mary asked her which town they were in, and she then said that she would see what she could do to help. After two days Sister Mary called Uzonna and told her that one of the reverend fathers from the church was travelling to Ubuli Ihejiofor, a town very close to the place where her brother and his family were staying. She said that she had asked him to give me a lift to Ubulu, and from there someone would help her to get to the place where her brother was staying, probably a reverend from Ubulu Presbytery.

It was a very exciting time for Uzonna, being able to join her family with the hope that her brother would be able to tell her where our stepmother was. She was going to be happy living with at least one member of the family. Little did she know that life would have been much better for her if she had stayed at the Roman Catholic camp.

The day came for the reverend father to travel, and he called and told her to gather everything she had. She put all her things in a paper bag, and off they went. The father drove as gently as ever, being stopped at every checkpoint and searched by the soldiers. In the end they reached the Ubulo market square. The reverend father asked one of the market women the way to Mr Andrew Awuka's compound, because they were told that Uzonna's family were staying there. The woman described the way to the house. When they got to Awuka's compound, the father asked the young man he saw at the compound to take them to Mr Awuka. He did so, and the father told him that he had brought Uzonna to see her brother and family, who were residing in his house. Mr Awuka called Uzonna's brother, who was very happy to see that she was still alive. He thanked the reverend father for bringing her to them. Uzonna's brother offered the father a sit and brought out some kola nut in accordance to the Ibo culture, which showed appreciation and welcome to visitors.

After the presentation of the kola nut, prayer was said, the kola nut was broken, and the reverend father took a piece, the remaining being passed around to others. After that the father took his leave and continued with his journey to the church he was supposed to visit.

Uzonna then went into the house and met her sister-in-law and her two sisters. Things seemed to be going fine for the first few weeks, and the three young girls worked together, fetching water and doing the housework together, and they all seemed to be happy with one another. As time went on, Uzonna noticed that her sister-in-law had started to show some sort of dislike towards her. It appeared that she was not happy seeing Uzonna and girls getting very close, like sisters. The woman then started fabricating stories that were not true about Uzonna, and she told her brother lots of lies against Uzonna. She said Uzonna had become very stubborn and refused to do some of the housework she told her to do. Uzonna's brother would then rebuke her very sternly, but most of the time the two other girls would come to her rescue, which their sister did not like. The wife warned them never to come to Uzonna's aid, or else she would throw them out of her house.

Things went on like that until one day Uzonna's sister-in-law called her, telling her that she was going to share the household chores among her and her two sisters. It was a surprise to Uzonna because the chores had always been done happily among the three girls with no complaint. Uzonna listened as her sister-in-law told her that she had to mop the whole house on Mondays and Fridays every week, wash all the dirty clothes for everybody in the house on Fridays, wash all dirty plates and cooking utensils after each meal every day, polish the floors every Saturday, and more. Uzonna was not angry or surprised because she did not know her sister-in-law did it intentionally in order to provoke her. Uzonna laughingly asked her sister-in-law, whom she called auntie, what her two sisters would be doing if she had to do all the house chores. Immediately her sister-in-law told her that she had no right to ask her how she shared the chores in her house. She said that she would teach Uzonna how to keep her mouth shut and never to tell her how to run the house. Uzonna did not think much of what she said and did not understand why her sister-in-law would get angry, because she did not disrespect her. Uzonna carried on with her domestic chores, singing as usual.

When it was lunch time, the three girls usually ate together out of the same bowl. However, her sister-in-law called her two sisters to come to carry their food. One of the girls called Uzonna and told her that their lunch was ready. Uzonna immediately heard the wife shouting at her sisters and telling them that Uzonna must not touch any part of the food, because she only gave them enough for two. One of the sisters said to her, 'But we always eat together with Uzonna.' The wife then shouted that if they ever challenged her instructions again, they would be stopped from eating any food.

The two sisters kept quiet, and one started to eat, but the other said that she was not going to eat if Uzonna was not allowed to eat with them. Efuru told the senior sister that Uche refused to eat because Uzonna was not allowed to eat. The senior sister asked her to call Uche for her, so Efuru called Uche for the senior sister. When Uche came, her sister asked her why she had refused to eat. Uche asked her older sister what Uzonna had done to deserve such punishment; Uzonna had been working very hard in the house and did not deserve to be punished. 'Uzonna has cleaned everywhere in the house, and washed all the dirty clothes. What else did you want her to do?'

Her senior sister told her that Uzonna had no right to tell her how to run her house, and that she did not like the way she ran her house, so she should the pack her things and leave her house, going to stay with her mother, knowing full well that Uzonna had no mother. Uche left her older sister and returned to the passage where Efuru was eating, but she did not eat herself.

Then during dinner time, the senior sister dished out the food, called Efuru to come and carry the food for her and her sister Uche. This time Efuru asked her older sister nicely if she could call Uzonna to eat with them, but she said no. As both girls were very hungry, they did eat. Uche tried to pass some food secretly to Uzonna, but Efuru, who was as wicked as her older sister, told Uche that if she ever did that, she would report her to their older sister, who then would take a very drastic action so that Uche could give any food to Uzonna.

Uzonna had not eaten any food for two days. It war time, and people did not have enough food to feed the family, so there was no chance for Uzonna to beg other families for food. Uzonna could not find anyone to give her food, so she then went into the bushes, picked up some pimpernel, cracked them, ate, and then plucked whatever fruits she could lay her hands on. She could not satisfy her hunger, and she cried herself to sleep.

On waking up, she saw her brother's car coming home. She gave sigh of relief, hoping that her brother would be able to persuade his wife to give her some food to eat. Uzonna greeted her brother, carried all the stuff in his car into the house, and prepared the bath for him to cool off. She then went to her sister-in-law and asked her if she could lay the table for her brother's food, which she had done ever since she lived with them. Her sister-in-law told her that her help was not needed and that it would be better for her to look for somewhere else to live. Uzonna did not understand what she was talking about, so she went out of the house and sat in the corridor. Uzonna's brother came out of the bedroom, and before Uzonna could say anything to him, he said with an angry voice to her, 'So you insulted my wife, just because she told you to do some housework?' Uzonna told him that she did not insult his wife, that she did all the things she was told to do in the house; if in doubt, he could ask Uche. But her brother did not listen to her and told her that his wife reported the incident to him, and the wife would not have told him lies. Uzonna was confused because she had not done anything to annoy her brother's wife and had not had any confrontation with her sister-in-law. She could not understand why the woman had made up the story, but she believed she wanted to find a way of justifying the starvation she inflicted on Uzonna.

Despite all that happened, Uzonna hoped that her brother would ask his wife to give Uzonna some food to eat. Instead he turned around and said to Uzonna that starvation was a small punishment for her behaviour, and that if not for what outsiders would say, he would ask her to leave his house because he hated the sight of her. He hoped would continue to starve until she collapsed. It was one of Uzonna's saddest days; she could not sleep all night, and all she did was think of what to do next or where to go, where she would get money to travel with and feed herself, and how safe it would be for her because she was still under age. Uzonna prayed so much that night.

She woke up that morning very early and did not have any purpose that day, so she just lay on the floor thinking. When the sun came up, Uzonna noticed that she had become a different girl. She had no fear in her anymore, no purpose for her living; life meant nothing to her. I could kill myself to make my brother, his wife, and others happy, and they would have no more responsibility of looking after me. Since I have no parents, no one would miss me if I die. My dying would be the end of my hunger, and the physical abuse I constantly receive from my brother, his wife, and other relatives. It then became a case of her leaving her brother's house, walking on the road and facing the possibility of being killed by a bomb, or being raped to death or killed by hunger. In her hearts of hearts, she was prepared to take any one of those things that came to take her; her only prayer was that whichever was to take her should take her quickly, not letting her suffer. She packed the little things she had into a plastic bag and headed to the gate to go.

As she walked to the gate, the landlord, who was coming back from his early morning visit to his sister, saw her and asked where she was going, with the bag in her hand and looking very sad. She told him that she was leaving the house. He asked why, and she tried to tell him, but tears rolled down her face. He came nearer and tried to console her, saying that she should tell him what the matter was, he would try his best to help. Uzonna then told him that her brother and his wife did not want her in their house anymore. The landlord asked her if it was her brother, and she said yes. He looked confused and said that she must be making a mistake. He believed that the man she called a brother was not her real brother—he could not believe a brother could allow his wife to treat his sister that way. He noticed that Uzonna did all the housework and never stopped fetching water and washing clothes. He hardly ever saw Uzonna playing like the wife's sisters. Uzonna told the landlord that she was very hungry and had not eaten for the past three days. The landlord took Uzonna to his sitting room, asked his wife to find some food for her to eat, and told Uzonna to wipe her tears. While his wife looked for food, the landlord went to the next house, where Uzonna's uncle and his family stayed. The landlord asked if truly the man Uzonna said was her brother was really her brother.

The uncle asked him why he'd ask such question. The landlord said it was to be sure because since the family had moved into his house, he had been noticing the wickedness he and his wife handed out to Uzonna, and he had thought Uzonna was just a house girl brought to be a slave for the family. The uncle told him that Uzonna was his tenant's youngest sister, who never knew their mother. The landlord was very angry and disappointed that a man who, he was told, was an engineer and studied in the United Kingdom could allow his wife to be that cruel to Uzonna.

On his return from the house, he noticed that Uzonna had eaten and looked a bit happy. He then asked her where she was going and if she had any money for transportation. She said that she had no money and was not very sure where she was going, but she would go to a town called Umuahia, where she had a cousin who lived there and was working with the food directorate. Uzonna's intention was to get to Umuahia before the close of work. She would ask the bus garage how to get to the office of the food directorate, and then she'd see her cousin and go home with her. The landlord gave her some money and asked his wife to find some dry snacks for her to take with, in case Uzonna was hungry on the road. He felt so concerned about me being on the road on my own, but he did say some prayers for her.

He then called Uzonna's brother and told him that he was greatly disappointed in him about how he and his wife had mistreated his own baby sister. He said, 'What type of a man are you?' He told him that since he and his family had moved into his compound, he had been noticing the wickedness he and his wife had been showing to this girl—his own sister! He said that he never would have believed that Uzonna was really his sister, if not for his uncle confirming the truth. He then told her brother that he must move out of his house within twenty-four hours. If the landlord did not know him before but could be kind to accommodate him and his family, how could the brother not show the same kindness to his own sister?

Uzonna left the compound. She thought of going back to her village; maybe she would find her stepmother and my youngest brother (a stepbrother). She could not find them in any of the camps, so they might have gone back to the village. Doing so was not possible because the sound of bombs could be heard very close to the village. She headed to Umuahia, walking to the market square to see the army trucks that came to buy some food and take it to different army camps. If she was lucky, she could see trucks going to Umuahia.

When she got to the market square, there were two trucks loading to go to Umuahia. She went to the officer who was in charge of one of them and asked him if he would allow her to travel to Umuahia in his truck. He looked at Uzonna and asked her with whom she was travelling. She said that she was travelling on her own. He said that it was dangerous for a girl to travel on her own, and asked Uzonna where her parents were. 'I have lost them,' she said. He then asked her who was going to meet her at Umuahia. 'I was going to stay with my cousin, who work with the office of the food directorate.' He asked if she knew how to get to the house. 'No, but when I get to the directorate, I will then go home with her.'

He said, 'What if the office is closed by the time we get there?'

'I would sleep in the compound until the next morning, when she comes to work.'

The officer said, 'It would be dangerous for you to sleep in the compound on your own. But do not worry; I will ask the security officers to look after you, should there be a need for you to sleep until the next morning. Bring your belongings here.'

Uzonna said, 'I have none—only what is in my hand.'

'Do you have money?'

'A kind landlord gave me some before I left his compound.'

'Why did you leave a secured place to travel to a place you do not know?'

She told him what had transpired between her brother and his wife. He felt sorry for her and told her to keep her money; he would look after her until they got to Umuahia.

It happened that the officer and his crew were going to the food directorate at Umuahia, where the food stuff was prepared and packaged into light bags for soldiers to take to the front lines. It was Uzonna's lucky day, the officer said, to be travelling with them. They might be able to solicit the help of her cousin to collect their rations of prepared snacks quickly, to enable them to return to Mgbidi early the next morning. The officer told her not to cry or worry, because he would ask her cousin to take good care of me.

Throughout the long journey, no one troubled Uzonna. She fell asleep on the way, which was good because she was saved from being hungry and thirsty. When she opened her eyes, the officer told her that they were almost at Umuahia, and that they would be there before half past four in the afternoon.

He gave Uzonna some water and a piece of bread to eat. She then began to look out of the window, admiring the scenery. The road was full of people coming and going from farms, streams, and the market. It was very exciting because Uzonna had never before travelled to Umuahia or been on a long journey on her own, except when they ran for their lives during the bombings. No one waited for each other, and everyone ran as fast as she could out of the danger zone. The only time people checked to see who made it safely was when no more bombs sounded.

After an hour and half, she was told that they were now at the outskirts of Umuahia. She was excited, anxious, and happy at the same time, looking forward to meeting her cousin. After half an hour, they were at the city, travelling towards the food directorate. At around 4.30 p.m. they were in front of a very big building with a massive gate and security men at both sides. One of the security men approached the truck. The driver stopped, got out of the truck, and went straight to the security man. Both exchanged greetings, and the driver showed the security man his documents. The security man took the documents back into the office for verification and then brought back the documents. The truck was also checked, and when the security man saw Uzonna, he asked the driver what the little girl was doing in the truck. The officer told the security man that the little girl was a relation of one of their officers, and they had brought her from Ubulu to see her. The security asked Uzonna who was her relation, and Uzonna told him. Straight away he opened the gate and asked the driver to drive into the compound. The security man then went to call Uzonna's cousin.

The security told the cousin that she had a visitor. The cousin asked the name of the visitor and where she came from. The security man told her that the little girl said her name was Uzonna, and that she came from Ubulu. The cousin could not believe her ears, so she came out running towards the truck. When she saw Uzonna, she shouted, 'How did you get here, and where did you get the money to pay for your transport? Why did you run away from your brother's house?'

'I did not run away,' Uzonna said, and then she could not hold her tears. She told her cousin that her brother and his wife threw her out of their house; the wife said that she could not stand having her in the house, and could not bear the feeling of feeding her with her sisters. 'My brother and his wife said that it would be better for them to throw me out of their house and put me on the street. Probably I would be killed by a bomb, and I would become one of those that lost their lives during the war, and then no one would blame them for my death.'

After telling her cousin all she remembered, the cousin asked her to bring her belongings. Uzonna showed her the tiny plastic bag she had in her hand. The cousin asked, 'Is it all you have?' Uzonna said yes. The cousin took it and opened it, looked into it, and said, 'Where are your other clothes?'

'That is all my clothes.'

The cousin then asked her again to tell her what happened. Uzonna repeated her story about the housework, the starving, and the beatings. She told her how the sisters tried very hard to tell my brother that Uzonna did not do any of the things their sister said she did, but the brother refused to listen.

The cousin was very angry with Uzonna's brother and his wife, especially because the brother met his wife through the cousin, when they were both teaching at the same secondary school and were very close friends. The cousin told her not to worry; she was happy to have her stay with her because she needed company. She also said that she would take good care of Uzonna.

At the close of work, they both went to the house. The cousin lived in a bed sitter with other tenants in the same house. All of them shared the kitchen, toilet, and bathroom. All tenants took it in turns to clean the toilet, the bathroom, and the compound. Whenever it was Uzonna and the cousin's turn, Uzonna made sure she cleaned everywhere very well. Living with the cousin was a very happy time for her. The cousin bought her more clothes and even got her some sandals. She was eating well and played with other children within the compound.

After a few weeks, the cousin came back from work and asked Uzonna if she would like to work in the kitchen in the Food Directorate, with other people helping out in the preparation of making dry packs for the Biafran soldiers. The dry packs were made from unripe plantains and bananas, peeled and cut into small, round circles, and then seasoned with hot peppers and salt, then fried really dry. They'd allow the basins to cool them, and they would be packed into small packs and sealed to prevent air from going into it and make it go soft. These were distributed to soldiers, especially those about to go to war fronts. It would be food to sustain them while at the front lines.

Uzonna said, 'Yes, I am excited. I have never worked before, so it is going to be a big challenge.' The cousin also told me that she was to receive seven pounds per month. It meant a lot to her, because she had never had money of her own, except for receiving a few pence from people for running errands. Now she was going to be paid monthly. Uzonna felt very grown up.

The following week she started my new job. She went with the cousin, who took her to the manager in charge of the kitchen, introduced them, and asked him to please take good care of her. Uzonna was underage, but she was not the only one in the kitchen. The cousin left, and they went to her office. The manager took her around, showed her were the ingredients were kept, and then took her to the supervisor and asked her to put Uzonna into a group.

The first day was wonderful, and she made friends immediately. People talked as they peeled, cut, and fried the plantain and banana chips. They were even allowed to eat as much as they wanted, and they were given some to take home. During the weekends they would be given some whole plantains and bananas to take home. After peeling and cutting, the basins of plantains and bananas were taken to the kitchen and seasoned, and then the older women would fry them while the younger women spread the mats where the fried chips would be poured, in order to allow them to cool before being packed into small plastic bags and then sealed for distribution. They packed the small packs into fifty-kilogramme jute bags for the soldiers. The army vehicles would come to pick up the jute bags and then take them to different units.

It was not an easy job, but that was one of the ways they could help the young men and women risking their lives while fighting the war, and it was a way for Uzonna to earn some money. No matter how small the money was, the fact was that she had enough food to eat.

It was a great change to her life, from starving to eating as much as she wanted, and meeting people from different parts of Biafra. She found out that some girls were in the same circumstances as she was, and that brought some comfort to her. It was very encouraging, because they were working for the army and had the privilege to be cared for whenever they were ill by the army doctors. After five weeks working in the kitchen, Uzonna received her first salary. It was great to be given an envelope with her name typed on top of it. She opened it and found seven one-pound notes—the first money she had ever earned. She was overjoyed and could not wait for the day to come to an end.

When it was seven in the evening, they were told to lock up. Everyone hurried up, locked the windows, packed up the frying pans, and then went home until tomorrow. Uzonna ran out, went home, and gave the whole money to her cousin, who had taken her into her one-bedroom accommodation, fed her, and helped her to get that job. The cousin was very impressed, opened the envelope, counted the money, took out three pounds, and gave Uzonna the rest of the money. She told her to buy herself a pair of sandals to use to go to work, so that she would stop using flip–flops, because it was not safe.

Things became brighter for Uzonna; she was even able to visit her brother and his wife, who starved her and threw her out of their house. The day she went to visit them, she carried a full bag of gari, two big bunches of plantains, and some yams. She was lucky to get a lift from one of the army vehicles that was travelling to Ubulu. The army vehicle was going to collect some food and equipments and was to travel back the next day. The cousin did ask the driver of the vehicle to take good care of Uzonna, and she also make sure that he returned the next day with her on board. It was never Uzonna's intention to ever see them or have anything to do with them, after they had treated her with such cruelty, but the cousin insisted that she visit them to show them that she was alive, and that the heavenly Father cared for everyone, both the rich and poor, the beautiful and ugly, the tall and short. God had a purpose for creating everything—human, animals, trees, rivers, and more—and God could make or destroy whomever he wanted.

Uzonna packed all her things together, and the following day they left Umuahia and travelled to Ubulu. The journey was an overnight journey. They got to Ubulu the following morning, and the driver made sure he took her to her brother's place. The first person she saw by the gate was the landlord. At first he could not make out who she was, because ever since she'd left the compound, she had never visited or kept in touch with anyone within the compound; they all thought she had died, as my brother wanted. They never made any attempt to find out if she was alive or dead.

When the landlord realised that it was Uzonna, he shouted and embraced her. The driver told him that she had a lot of things in the vehicle and would need help to carry them out. The landlord was very excited, ran into the compound, and called her sister-in-law's sisters to come. When they came out and saw her, they could not believe their eyes. They hugged each other, and tears rolled down Efuru's eyes. She said that she thought Uzonna had already died, but now that she had seen me, she was very happy. Uzonna told them that she had lots of things inside the vehicle. They started carrying out the things, and the sisters were very surprised to see the bag of gari, huge plantain bunches, bananas, and stock fish, which was a very rare commodity to come across during the war. They asked Uzonna how she managed to buy those things, where she was staying, and how come she was looking very well. Uzonna told them how she travelled to Umuahia and that she was staying with her auntie Nnonye, who had been taken good care of her and was the one that helped to secure her a job at the Food Directorate.

The landlord said that Uzonna must be mentally ill to bring all those things to the husband and wife who wanted her dead. She told him that she knew what she was doing; she only wanted to prove to them that she was alive, was well cared for, and was able to make enough money to pay them back any money they spent on her. In fact it was to show them that they could not control or hold onto her life, because her living and dying belonged to God Almighty.

As the girls carried all the commodities into the kitchen, their sister asked them where all the things came from, wondering if her husband had returned early from work. The girls said no, her husband had not returned. As they carried all the products into the kitchen, the brother returned from his work, saw all the products, and asked where they came from. Uzonna then came forward and told him that she'd brought all the things to repay him and his wife for whatever food they gave her while she was with them.

She told him that she was not going to ever stay with him and his wife, and nothing would ever make her come to their house again. Uzonna went to stay with the landlord and his family. The landlord's wife fed her, and they had a very nice chat before they went to bed. The following morning the driver and the soldiers came to pick Uzonna up for their return journey to Umuahia. Uzonna said good-bye to the landlord and his family before the truck drove away from the compound on its way back. It was a very smooth and enjoyable journey back to Umuahia. The driver picked up some passengers on their way back, and they were good company to Uzonna, chatting all the way back to Umuahia.

The truck got back to Umuahia very late in the evening, and Uzonna felt very tired. She told her cousin all that had happened on the way, then they went to bed. In the morning they got ready and went to work. At work they brought out the plantain and unripe bananas to start peeling, slicing, season, and then fry.

They heard the noise of falling bombs and guns and people shouting. The workers all came outside to see what was going on and saw people running and shouting, 'Run for your life!. They ran back to the kitchen, collected their bags, ran outside, and joined others to run home. When Uzonna got home, she saw her cousin already packing her clothes and some food into a bag. Uzonna packed the little things she had acquired and some food as well. They had to pack as much as they could carry because we did not know how far they were to run before they could stop. They all came out and followed the others to run to safety as the bombs and jet fighters were shooting everywhere and killing people. They ran until the noise stopped, sat down for a while, got their breath back, and then got up. The survivors started taking care of all the dead bodies. It was very sad to see that some of the people they were talking with while running were dead, but they had to do what they could to survive.

The group managed to dig a massive grave and buried the bodies. They collected some of the dead people's things that were useful and took them for themselves. because if they did not do so, the next group of people that came round would. At the end of everything, when they noticed that things had become quiet, they returned to the Food Directorate building and went into the kitchen area—only to find that there was nothing like a kitchen anymore. The whole compound was burnt to the ground. Then they heard the Biafran soldiers driving up and down the street, using a microphone and telling everyone to evacuate the town because the Nigerian soldiers would definitely return. Once they started bombing and shooting a town, it was a sign that they were coming near to the place, and they would do everything within their power to capture the town. Whenever they entered any town, they would rape and kill all the women.

The survivors ran out of the town, as far away as possible. That was the second chapter of the beginning of Uzonna's suffering, with no job and no shelter. Uzonna's cousin had gone to find where her directorate had moved, and a driver was sent to pick her up with the other top officials; it was their duty to find a safe town to relocate. Uzonna was then left on her own again.

Uzonna then joined the others as they all ran into the middle of this thick bush to hide from the Nigerian soldiers. They used their bare hands to clear the bush, break some leaves from the trees, and then spread out some clothes on top of the leaves to make beds. After that they started to look for somewhere to fetch water with which to drink and cook. It was very difficult because no one knew where they were or which way to go to find the river. Nonetheless, they started searching everywhere within the forest. They divided ourselves into two groups and said that if any group should come across a river or any flowing water, it should alert the other. All the fears of wild animals vanished from their hearts because they were very thirsty and hungry.

After a very long search, they finally found a small stream running down a valley. There was great relief as they all drank water, washed their faces, and then filled their containers with water to take back to the shelter. When they got back, they cooked the cornmeal they'd brought with them after gathering some firewood in the forest. They had their first meal after three long days of going without food, and they regained some strength.

After they had eaten, they sat around in a big circle. It was very dark, and they had no light because no one came with a lamp. The older people within the group told some stories, such as why the war started, and how brothers, sisters, and parents were killed by their Moslem brothers in the North, who called the Southerners nyamiri (infidel). The Moslems destroyed all the businesses of the Southerners in the North, and hence the Southerners decided to break away from Nigeria because they felt that they were not wanted within Nigeria. The Northerners were advised by the British not to allow the Southerners to break away, because most of Nigerian wealth came from the South. The war started as the then Nigerian government wanted to keep the South within Nigeria just for economic purposes. The British then supplied Nigeria with arms, and some mercenaries came to enable them to defeat Biafra.

After two days, news came to the group that they were very lucky to have left Umuahia, because the Nigerian soldiers did demolish every building in that town and killed all the people who were left.

The survivors slept in the thick forest for a week, and then they ran out of food. They did not how far they were from the nearest town or village, to find a market to buy food. They had to keep drinking water, but on third day they were very hungry and the younger children among us started to fall ill. The group decided to do something, even though they knew it was very risky. They split into groups and then started combing different parts of the bush, looking for something to eat. The men chased any moving thing they laid their eyes on; they caught some lizards, snakes, and squirrels. The women brought some wild fruits. Everyone gathered some firewood, made a fire, and roasted all the animals and the wild fruits, eating every bit of it. They drank the water they had fetched and we regained their strength.

The following day after a long sleep, the group decided to come out of the forest gradually, to make sure there were no Nigerian soldiers around. Then they would walk as far as they could until they found a town with human beings. They trekked for two days and then heard voices. They ran into the bush, listening to make sure the voices were speaking in Igbo. What a relief to hear people speaking in Igbo, and to know that at last they were in a town! It was agreed that just one person would go out, one who spoke Hausa, Yoruba, and Igbo, in case the people in the town were not Ibos.

Mazi Ude agreed to go out, and then returned to tell us that they were in a town called Nsulu, in Isi Ala Ngwa, which was on the Biafra side. They were happy and came out of hiding. Uzonna had two cousins who were working there. Straight away she went to look for them at their work place, before the close of work, because she had no idea where they lived. Luckily she managed to find them and went home with them.

When they got to her place, she gave Uzonna soap to have a bath and gave her a change of clothes and some proper food to eat. The following morning she asked Uzonna to go her to her workplace because the employers were recruiting new workers. She went for the recruitment, completed the forms, and was short-listed. The next day was interview day. Uzonna was there on time and very excited, waiting for her turn.

Three girls went in before her. She noticed that when each came out, she was adjusting her dress, but Uzonna did not think much of it; it may be from the way they sat on the chair. She went in and greeted the interviewer, and then he offered a chair and asked some questions. She answered, and he even said that she answered very well. He then asked when she would like to start. Uzonna said immediately and thanked him as she got up to go. He called her back and said to go through the other door.

Uzonna asked, 'Which way?'

He said, 'To the bedroom.'

'My question is for what?'

'Did your cousin not tell you what you were to give, to get the job?' Uzonna said no. He said, 'Everyone does it.'

'You mean all the girls have to sleep with you to be offered a job?' He said yes. 'I will think about it and come back tomorrow.'

Uzonna went home and told her cousin what happened. She said that was how it went—every worker went through the same thing. Uzonna asked what if they got pregnant. The cousin said no one got pregnant, because there was something they had to use after sleeping with the old man: a full litre of kaikai (illicit jin). Uzonna was very frightened because kaikai burnt like paraffin—how could one drink a whole litre? She decided not to be a part of it. She'd rather have no job than sleep with a man who was even older than her father. What if after sleeping with the old man, she drank the kaikai, and it destroyed her life, or what if she did not drink it and got pregnant? She would then kill herself. I can't get someone to care for me as single girl.

How much more difficult will it be if I became a pregnant teenage girl?

It was a very hard decision to make. Uzonna got up the next morning and told her cousin that she was not going to go ahead with the plan. The cousin was angry with me and asked how Uzonna was going to feed herself. She said that Uzonna was not better or younger than the other girls who did the same thing and got the jobs, so if she was not prepared to sleep with the old man and get the job, she should get out of the room because the cousin could not afford to feed her.

It was a very difficult time for Uzonna, but it was much better to die from hunger than to die trying to abort a baby. she picked up the few things she'd acquired during the time she was working with the Food Directorate. It was very early in the morning, so she left the cousin's house and came out to the main road. She saw lots of people walking aimlessly, and she joined the crowd. Everyone continued to walk, heading to another village until it became dark. They all gathered into an empty school building and passed the night there.

In the morning the group woke up and went to look for running water, to have a bath and drink. They had to trek a very long distance before they found a stream. They had a bath, took some water back to the school to use in cooking, and prepared whatever they could find for food before they continued to explore the area. To Uzonna's surprise, she found out that she was very close to Ubulu, where her brother and his family was staying. She did not want to go back to them, and surely they would not want her back, so she continued the journey with those who were still moving on.

They came to a market, and how lucky they were, because they were able to beg for things. People were very generous and gave them lots of food. They felt very sorry for them because the survivors looked like aliens from another world and had been walking for several days. The group asked if there was a stream around, and the villagers showed the way to the stream. It was then that Uzonna thought of returning to Obosi, as she learnt that her stepmother and little brother were there. It would be better for her to be with her stepmother than sleeping with an old man. She had had very bad experiences with the people she trusted.

Though the odd bombs did fall at Obosi, people who were staying there already knew how to take cover. Most families built their own bunkers to take refuge in until everything calmed down. Some families who did run out of Obosi the first time had returned due to the hardships they were passing through at the places they were taking refuge. Most of the people staying at Obosi had mastered the timing of when the shells fell in the village. Uzonna felt that if those people were living and surviving at Obosi, why should she not join them? If she returned to the village, she might be lucky enough to find her stepmother, and it would be easier to find food; she could plant some vegetables, some cassava, and some yam. There was a good stream, and she would be staying in a place she knew very well. She headed to Obosi with some of her friends who were also from Obosi. It took them fifteen days to get to the bridge head at Oba, which was very close to Obosi.

When they got there, they had to stop because they did not know when the next bombs would occur. They waited to see if anyone was coming from Obosi, as many of the Obosi residents usually came to Oba to buy some food items. They went into the river, had a bath, and drank some clean water. The bridge head was the major road leading into Obosi, but there were other bush paths mainly known by the elders of Obosi, and many of them used the hidden footpaths to escape from Obosi whenever the Nigerian soldiers came into the town to search for people and food.

They were all hiding within the bush by the river and remained there until late in the evening. They then saw two men coming out from the bush near the river. At first no one made a sound because the group was not sure who they were—they might have been Nigerian soldiers dressed as civilians, pretending to be from Obosi to find out where Biafran soldiers were or to see if they could find any settlements of Biafran civilians. The refugees were watching them as they came nearer towards the side. One of the women ran out of the hidden bush and ran towards the men, shouting, 'It is my husband!' and she hugged him. It was a very emotional reunion because they had been separated for over a year, each one not knowing that the other was alive. Everyone came out of the hiding place. The woman who shouted was called mama Nkiru, and her husband and his friend asked everyone to come out of the bush and follow them to the village.

They told the group that they should not talk aloud, because the place was not far Onitsha where the Nigerian Soldiers were stationed. It was about a forty-five-minute walk, but they got to the village safely. The two men asked each person his family name, telling us if it was safe to go to the houses or not. Those whose houses were near Onitsha were told not go back there, because any slightest noise or smoke coming out of the kitchens would alert the Nigerian soldiers.

In that case Uzonna was not able to return to her father's house, and she had to find somewhere to stay. She decided to go right into the village to her friend's house, right inside the village, to see if she could find anyone in the house. When she got to their house, she was very lucky to find the whole family; apparently they all returned to the village when things became very difficult for the family. They were happy to see her. She told them all she went through with her brother and his wife. They encouraged her to stay with them.

Uzonna settled within the family very quickly because they treated her as if she was one of them. She followed them whenever they went to fetch firewood from the neighbouring town, Umuoji. They would then walk across a shallow river to get to the side where the bush was, and they would cut as much wood as they would carry to get home. The journey was quite far, so they would leave the house around four in the morning and would not return until around eight at night. It was safer to return around that time, because it was dark and quiet, so if there were any intruder, they would know and then hide until it was safe. They sold the firewood to people who could not go get some, and the money would be used to buy some food.

One day when things seemed to be quiet, when it was dark, Uzonna went to her father's compound, only to see that our house had been levelled to the ground by a bomb. Most nights she would go there and search through the rubble to see if she could find anything valuable. Sometimes she was able to find something, and one day she found an Ovaltine tin. She opened it to see if the contents were still all right. To her surprise it was full of money. It was her stepmother's money that she got from the sale of her utaba. It was a lot of money, so she took it and showed it to her friend's mother, who told Uzonna to keep the money carefully and make sure no one would steal it; they might need it in the future. The money was enough for the family to buy food for two to three months.

The family continued to fetch firewood to sell, to make sure that they were well fed. They continued with this routine until one day the older people decided that they should all go to Otuocha to buy a large quantity of food and other household requirements, come back, and then sell some of them. It would help them to forget the war, only being reminded when they heard the shooting from Onitsha.

Uzonna had not heard of the place, so she asked her friend Chinwe how far the place was, how many days walk, and how safe it was to trek to the town. Chinwe replied that it was safe, it was two days' journey, and they would be surprise to see many of our classmates there. She said that many people went there to purchase goods to sell, in order to make a living. Chinwe said that she had gone there many times and would go with whenever they were to go.

That gave Uzonna more confidence, though the journey could sometimes be risky, because sometimes they would have to dodge bullets coming from the neighbouring town. When that happened, the journey would take longer because they would have to take cover for safety for the day and then continue the following day. However, going with Chinwe made the whole trip happier for Uzonna. Chinwe had the experience and would be in a position to advise what goods to buy, what would be sold quicker, and what would give more profit.

The next day the family came out around four in the morning and had some roasted yam with palm oil, and also calabash full of drinking water for the journey to Otuocha. When it was dark, they would walk by the main road, but when the day broke, they would walk in the bushes to avoid being seen by the enemy. It was not an easy journey—it was very tiring and exhausting. At times they all sat in the middle of the forest to eat roasted yams and drink some water, to have some rest and refresh their strength, and then continued on our journey. On the second day they met up with some other villagers going to Otuocha.

To Uzonna's surprise her stepmother was with the group. She screamed with joy when she saw her, and immediately someone held her mouth so as not to alert the enemies. The stepmother was happy to see her and asked where she had come from. Uzonna told her that she was staying with Chinwe and her family. The stepmother asked her how she had been surviving, and she told her that since she had come to Obosi, Chinwe and her parents had looked after her. Uzonna's stepmother said that she must go home with her. They all went together, and on their return, Uzona went home with her stepmother to wherever she was staying.

She told her stepmother how she had been visiting the house during the night to search for valuables, and how she had found the tin containing money from the sale of utaba, and she had been using the money carefully. The stepmother said that she was very happy that Uzonna had found the money instead of another person finding it. She asked her about her younger brother, and her stepmother told her that he was staying with her but could not join her on the journey to Otuocha, because he was too young to do so.

The third day they were getting very near to Otuocha, and they stopped and listened to the surroundings to make sure bullets were not coming. Luckily it was calm, one of the quiet periods, so they continued their journey into Otuocha. On reaching the market at Otuocha, Uzonna bought as much salt as she could carry, some black-eyed beans, some brown beans, and some dried fish. They all bought some ukpo ogede to eat on the way back to Obosi.

Ukpo ogede was made from corn and ripped plantain, like a cake, and it could last for days without spoiling. At the close of the market in the evening, they were on their way back to Obosi. The load we carried was quite heavy, so they stopped several times to have some rest.

They arrived at Obosi, but it was a very difficult time for Uzonna. She collected her belongings and moved to stay with her stepmother and brother. She had a mother again, and she was always very loving and caring. They sold everything we wanted to sell and made triple profit on all the things they bought. The stepmother moved back to the father's old compound, which was right inside the village and very spacious. They started farming again, planting some yam, cassava, vegetables, plantains, and bananas; they were able to feed themselves from the garden produce within six months. Things became much better for them in the village; the only problem they had was not being able to see Uzonna's sisters and other brothers, who lived abroad. Life seemed a bit normal in the village.

One morning as they were getting ready to go about usual duties, there was a very loud noise all over the village. People ran around, trying to find out what was going on. They heard that Biafra had surrendered. One could not imagine the situation. Some people went out to the main road to verify what was happening. It was a mistake for the women, who followed the men to venture outside. The Nigerians had covered all the roads within the village; they were going from house to house, bringing men out of the houses and killing them while the women were raped and killed. The few men that escaped ran through the bush, came back, and told everyone to run into the bush and hide. The Nigerian soldiers entered the village from Port Har Court. Uzonna's family left whatever they were doing, though they managed to grab some of their wrappers, and they ran for their lives back into the very thick forest, where no one entered. They did not think of dangerous animals that lived in the forest. No one could predict how long they were going to be in that forest.

The first night in the forest was very difficult. They could not sleep and were afraid of animals within the forest—and most of all of the Nigerians—but the night passed without any incident. When the morning came, they walked around the forest looking for something to eat and drink. They spent three nights in the forest before word came round that the head of state, General Yakubu Gown, had given an order that all soldiers must return to barracks and stop killing and raping women. He said that any soldier found engaging in these evil acts would face the firing squad. Gradually soldiers cleared from the street. When it looked like the street was calm, the very old men went to the street to see what was happening. They came back and asked the other men to come home with them, but the women should stay until they returned again. The women and girls spent an extra night within the forest. The following day some of the men came to tell all the women to return to their houses, because things had settled down in the village.

Uzonna went home, and the family had to locate again. Her father's house had been levelled to the ground. The first thing they did was build a shed where they could sleep. Hunger began to bite, and they had no money to buy food. The Biafran money was not acceptable by Nigerian traders. It was a very difficult time; everyone had to think fast. Uzonna remembered the relief centre they used to go to before they vacated the village, so she went there to find out if they had come back to help the villagers.

On getting there, Uzonna met one of the workers. He recognised Uzonna and called her by her name. Uzonna ran and embraced him, and he said, 'So you survived? Where are your brother and stepmother? Are they alive?'

Uzonna said, 'Yes, but we are very hungry. We have no food, or money to buy some food.'

He went into the store, came back with a jute bag, and asked Uzonna if she would be able to carry the bag home. Uzonna took the heavy bag from him, opened it, and found that the bag was filled with lots of different food stuffs: stock fish, cornmeal, cooking oil, packets of salt, oats, rice, beans, and powdered egg yokes. Uzonna was very happy, and tears of happiness fell from her eyes. Though the bag was very heavy for Uzonna, she managed to carry it home. When she got home, her stepmother was very happy. They cooked some of the cornmeal with corned beef, and the food lasted for more than a week. The relief did tell her to come back any time they need more food. She even got some soap from the relief centre. The amount of cornmeal she got from the relief centre was a lot, and Uzonna decided to make something out of it to sell it and make some Nigerian money, so that they would be able to buy things they needed. Uzonna then mixed some of the cornmeal with water, pounded some pepper into it, added some salt, smashed some ripped bananas, and mixed everything together. She made it into lots of balls and fried them with some of the cooking oil.

The people that were passing through saw her frying them, stopped, and asked what it was. She told them that it was something one could use to have pap for breakfast in the morning; pap was made from ground corn and was a white custard. They asked how much she was selling them, and she told one ball for a penny. They bought one, tried it, and found out that it was very tasty, so they bought more. The news went round that Uzonna was making something that was very good for breakfast, so more and more people came to buy it. She sold quite a lot and realised that she made good money. Since then Uzonna made up her mind that she would start doing that in greater quantity. She went back to the relief centre to see if she could get more corn, only to find out that the centre had closed due to an order received from the federal government. Now she had to use some of the money she made to buy the corn and other things.

Uzonna went to their back garden and was lucky to find a banana tree with some ripe bananas on it. She cut them down and carried the bunch into the shade. She then used some of her money to buy corn. She would soak the dried corn in hot water overnight, and very early in the morning she would carry the soft corn to a place where the grinding was done for a payment of a few pennies, because everyone was looking for Nigerian money. After grinding she would then carry it home; mix it with mashed bananas, pepper, and salt; and then fry them. It was called banana fritters. Uzonna found out that she could make enough money for the family to survive on, until they knew what would happen to the defeated Biafrans. Uzonna carried on with her trade, until one day a friend of hers who usually visited her every day came round and introduced a Nigerian soldier as a friend. Uzonna used some of the fritters to give them as kola, they ate them, and after they had finished, the soldier asked Uzonna what her future plan was.

Uzonna told him that she would be selling the fritters until she made enough money to pay her school fees. She would then go back to school to sit for her certificate examination, and maybe she'd sit for some O-level examinations. She said that she would like to go into university if one of her brothers who lived in the UK would pay her university fees. He then asked me what class she was before the war broke out. She told him that she was in her fourth year of secondary school. He put his hand into his pocket and gave her twenty pounds, which was a lot of money at that time. He told her to use the money to pay for transportation to Abgor, where he was based in Delta State. He said that he knew of a very good secondary school, where he could get her admitted to continue with her education. Uzonna asked him why he was doing this for her. He said that her friend had told him everything about me—how much she had suffered, and that she had no one to help her.

It was a dream come true for Uzonna. The next two days she packed up her fritter frying, gathered the few things she had acquired, put them into a plastic bag, gave some money to her brother and stepmother, said good-bye to them, and travelled to Agbor in Delta State, to meet up with her friend's friend. The soldier would take her to the secondary school, register her, and pay her school fees as promised. It was a very long and tedious journey because the roads were destroyed during the war. By the time she got to Agbor, it was dark, but she managed to get to the address he'd given her.

When she got to the house, the man welcomed her and was very hospitable. He took her into the spare room in his house and told her to keep her things there. He then showed her the bathroom and told her to freshen up; when she finished, she should come out to eat something. Uzonna did as she was told, and after she had eaten, she thanked him. She became a bit worried because she had seen his wife and children, whom he told she was going to stay with on her arrival. She asked him about his family, and he said that his wife and children had gone to see their grandmother and would be on their way, returning to the house. She said that he should thank them and his wife for being so kind to someone they had never met before. Uzonna was very tired from her long journey, and she said good night to him and went straight to bed. It did not take for her long to fall asleep, and she had hoped that the family would have returned while she was sleeping. She had it in her mind to apologise to his wife in the morning for not being able to stay awake to thank her.

As she slept, she could feel someone's hand touching her thighs. At first it was like in a dream, but it continued, so she jumped up only to find the man on her bed. She was very frightened and asked him what he was doing. He said that he wanted to find out if she was all right. She said that she was fine, and he could go back to his room and allow her to sleep—but he would not go. He continued to forcefully rip her clothes from her body. She begged him to let her go, saying that if this was the price for getting back into secondary school, she would not do it. She told him she would rather trek back to her village the following day and continue with her fritters, but he would not let go.

She told him that she would scream and wake his family up. He then laughed and told her that he was only lying when he told her that she was coming to stay with his family. His family was not there and stayed in their home town.

He raped her over and over again. She thought of killing herself because life meant nothing anymore. She went through the same experience she had when she was gang-raped by five men: she felt dirty and useless, and had lost every hope in living. Uzonna could no longer sleep throughout the night and cried all night, her body shaking like jelly.

The soldier went back to his room while she sat in a corner behind the door of the room, very frightened that he would come back again. He did not come back, but she could not go back to that filthy bed, so she sat at corner until daybreak. In the morning, after he had had his bath, he asked his house help to prepare some breakfast. He came to the door of the room and noticed that she did not close it as he told her. H could not see her on the bed, so he was a bit worried. He called her name and asked if she was in the bathroom, but she did not answer and was still uncontrollably shaking. He started looking at every corner and then saw her sitting behind the door. He felt so sad and worried and started to beg her to please not to be afraid; he knew that what he did to her was wrong, but he could not stop himself. He said he would do anything she wanted, but she should please stop crying and shaking. He begged her to have a bath and eat some breakfast. He went back into his room, came back with a big bag, and gave it to her.

She told him that she did not want anything from him. The only thing she wanted was for him to open the door let her go back to her village. He asked who she was going to stay with, if she went back to the village. Uzonna told him that her stepmother was there. He said that the stepmother would not be able to send her to school. She told him that she knew that, but if going to school would result in being raped, she would rather not go back to school and continue with her little business in the village, until one of her brothers got in touch with her again.

He could see how distressed she was. He went back to his room, returned, and gave her two tablets and begged her to take them if she did not want to be pregnant. He brought some water for me, and she took the tablets. She managed to have a bath, and when she came out of the bathroom, she saw a bag on the bed. Uzonna looked into it and noticed that it was full of clothes. He knocked on the door, and she ran very fast into the bathroom and locked the door. He begged her to open the door and said that he only came to tell her that he bought some clothes for her, and that she should use them. She did not open the door until she was sure that he had left the room. She had no other clothes, so she put on one of the outfits he'd bought.

She then came out of the room with the bag and told him that she was ready to go to the bus garage, to return to the village. He said that he would come with his driver to take her to the bus station. He asked her to eat something, but she refused and just stood by the door, waiting for his driver. When he could not get her to eat, he called his driver, who brought out the car. They got into the car. She never said a word, though he never stopped talking to me, pretending that nothing happened. She did not know the town, so she thought that they were going to the bus station. She only found out later that they drove to the secondary school. She told him that she was no longer interested in going back to school. He pleaded with her to forgive him for his horrible behaviour and promised that he would never do that to her or to any other girl, and that he would help her.

She got out of the car, and the driver drove off. She saw a big gate with bold writing on top of the gate: 'Girls High School, Agbor'. She was greeted by the principal, who offered them a seat. The soldier told the principal that Uzonna was the girl he'd spoken about. The principal asked her for her name and what year she was in secondary school before the war started. Uzonna told her that she was in year four. The principal told her that she had registered me in year five. The soldier then gave the principal the school fees and some more money, which he said was to be kept for Uzonna in case of an emergency, and for school trips and pocket money. He then turned round to her, gave her a large sum of money, told her to use it to buy the things listed in the prospectus, and good-bye. He left the office, went to his car, and then left.

The principal called one of the school prefects and asked her to take Uzonna to the dormitory and show her around the school compound. She did as the principal instructed her and asked Uzonna her name. She said she was sorry to hear of the things that had happened to refugees during the war. Uzonna told her that it was very kind of her to sympathise, but they had to forget about the war now and look to the future.

Uzonna asked her if it would be possible for her to go out of the school to go and buy bedding, provisions, and toiletries.

She said that the principal already told her that Uzonna was allowed to do so because she came with none of the required necessities. Uzonna asked her how to get to the market. She then called two of the older school girls to go with her and show her to the market.

They went to the market, and Uzonna bought most of the important things she needed. She tried to save some money because she knew then that it was going to be very difficult for her to get more money. She paid for a taxi to take them back to school, and they also had some fruit juice on the way back—Uzonna's way of saying a thank-you to the two girls for going with her to the market.

Uzonna started school in another state, away from the broken school buildings in the East. Going back to school after three years, during which time the country had the most horrible civil war, was very difficult, and it took her some time to settle down. There was always terrible nightmares, bad dreams, episodes of going through periods of depression, and remembering many of the handsome, hard-working young men that lost their lives during the war. The most terrible thing was to know that they died for nothing because Biafra was defeated in the war. There was never going to be memorials for them, no compensations to their families, and there would be nothing to honour them. She had lots and lots of sleepless nights, but as time went by, things became better. In a way she was lucky because she was in the same class with a girl who used to be in the same school before the war started. The girl was Uzonna's school daughter at the time and came from Delta State; when the war broke out, she returned to her original state with her parents. The girl was in year two while Uzonna was in year four, but now both were in year five. Uzonna thought that she was going to take the mick out of her, but to her surprise she was very supportive towards her and tried so hard to help. Whenever the girl saw her sitting very quiet, she would come and give her some words of encouragement, asking if Uzonna needed anything. Uzonna asked her why she was being so kind, and the girl told her that when Uzonna was her school mother, she treated her very well, just like a little sister. She told Uzonna how she used to stand up for her, buy her what she did not have, and protect her from the school bullies.

Whatever the girl noticed that Uzonna did not have, she would give it to her, knowing that Uzonna had a very limited amount of money. In fact the people of Delta State were very generous towards all the students that returned from Biafra, because they knew that they returned empty–handed; Biafra money was not acceptable within Nigeria. The school did not ask the students who returned from Biafra to pay their school fees, but told them that at the end of the year, if they wanted to collect their school certificates, they then had to pay their fees. That was very kind of them because no one would be driven out of school for not paying school fees. That helped a lot of students who returned from Biafra to finish their studies without disruptions. The school was a Baptist secondary school, and most of the teachers and the school principal were all Americans. They even provided most student with school textbooks and asked them to deposit the books into the school library at the end of the year.

Though part of Uzonna's school fees were paid by the soldier, she could not pay the remainder of the fees. She thought that her older brother, who was living in the United Kingdom during the time of the war, would return home and might be able to pay the remainder of her school fees, but that was not the case. When he came to Nigeria after the war, there was so much for him to do, and the most important was to build a house for the family so they could have a roof over their heads. It was very difficult for him to do everything, and in the end Uzonna left Nigeria without her school certificate.

Coming to the UK did not stop her from continuing with her education. She never received the certificate, and now it would be obsolete. Uzonna tried so hard to get the certificate, and she sent some money to the school for postage, writing several times, but to no avail. The fact that she did not receive the certificate did not hinder her from getting other qualifications. After her secondary education, she wanted to further my education by going into one of the universities in Nigeria, but due to her poor result, she only got a grade three. Though she passed eight subjects, she failed math. For one to get admission into any Nigerian university, one must have at least a grade of C in math and English. Uzonna was able to get admission into one of the vocational colleges, with the help of her older sister's neighbour, who was a lecturer in the institution. She studied cosmetology to become a beautician. The institution was where her sister and husband lived, so she had to move to Enugu to live with them. Her brother-in-law did not like this course in any way; he said that it was not a course for a young girl.

One day they practised manicures, and she returned home with her toe nails painted. The brother-in-law went mad, shouted at her, and told her that she must remove the paintings or else she could not enter the house. Uzonna did not have any nail polish remover, nor did she know where to get one; it took her a very long time to scrape all of it from her toes with a razor blade. He said that Uzonna was only studying to become a prostitute, and if that was the only course she could get to do, she should then stop going to college and find something else to do, because she would not live in his house and attend such a course. In a way he did not want her to live with them, but he did not know how to say it, so he was looking for every excuse to send her back to the village. When Uzonna's older brother, who lived in the UK, called, the brother-in-law told him that she was studying to become a prostitute and was embarrassing him.

Uzonna's brother and his wife were looking for someone to help them look after their children and help with housework. Her brother and her sister had a long talk, and in the end the brother said that he would take Uzonna back to London with him as their house girl. She was over the moon—getting out of Nigeria was like getting out of a high-security prison. She was physically, emotionally, and sexually abused during the war, and after the war living with the sister and attending college was a nightmare. Her sister's husband was very wicked and abusive and had no regard for anyone. He did not want her living with them because he would always comment that Uzonna was eating the food in the house for free, though she did a lot of housework and looked after the children. Her sister could not say or do anything because she was very much terrified of her husband. She could see what I was going through but could not do anything to stop it.

Her sister's husband was a very domineering man. He harassed Uzonna's twin sister and Uzonna a lot sexually, but they could not tell anyone about it because no one would believe them. When her brother agreed to take her to London, Uzonna twin sister decided to go back to the village to take a break For Uzonna, going to London was a dream come true. Her brother and told her the news, but he warned her of the difficulties—the cold weather and the loneliness. He told her a bit about the food and the housework she would be doing, and he said that when she got to London, his wife would show her the rest of her responsibilities. He then went to apply for a visa for her. He wanted her to come to London as a student, but he could not get a student visa; in the end his mother-in-law managed to get Uzonna visa as a house girl. She had to travel on her own because her brother and his wife had already left Nigeria before all arrangements for her travel was completed.

The flight was booked. Her brother's mother-in-law told her that when she went into the plane, she should quietly read the newspaper she would be given. She should never take anything from anyone, and never carry any luggage for anyone even if she know them. She said that the brother would come to the London airport to pick her up.

On the travelling day, Uzonna went to the airport in Lagos, checked in, and was given her seat number. She waved good-bye to her sister-in-law's mother and her brother, who brought her to the airport. She sat down, waiting to be called to board the plane. In about half an hour the passengers were called to board. She had never gone into the plane before, and she followed the other passengers. She did not know what she was going to see, but to her surprise she noticed that the plane was just like entering the train. She looked for her seat number, found it, and sat down, watching others as they went to their allocated seats. The doors were shut, and the demonstrators stood up and asked everyone to listen and watch. Passengers were shown and told of all the emergency measures, in case there was need for that. After the demonstration, they were told to put on seatbelts and relax; the plane was about to take off.

When the plane reached a certain attitude, they were told that they could watch the televisions. Uzonna had never seen this before, so she called for assistance to have the TV switched on. An air hostess did it for her with a smile; she even asked if Uzonna was all right. In Uzonna's mind she was already going to heaven—she had never been treated so nicely. They were given food and drink, and some papers to read.

Upon getting to London, the pilot announced that they would be landing in few minutes time. Uzonna was very excited as they were again reminded to fasten seatbelts because the plane was landing. They did so, and she could feel the plane tilting lower and lower toward the ground. Finally they landed at Heathrow Airport. They left the plane and then came to an area where they had to queue up for their documents to be checked. After checking they would then come out to go to their respective destinations.

When Uzonna was coming out, she was stopped by the security men, who asked her to give them her passport. She did give it to them, and they kept looking at the photograph in the passport and looking at my face. One of them said that she was not the one on the photo on the passport, and she told them that it was her. She was taken into a room, where a higher officer was just about to interview her. Then her brother walked in with an officer, who told them to let her go. Her passport was taken from her and stamped, 'Not allowed to take part in any type of job, even domestic duties.' If she did not go into full-time studies within three months, she would be sent back home. In the end she was allowed to go with her brother.

She was very cold, and her lips were shaking because she only had a very light cardigan. Within a short time they were inside her brother's car, and the car had a heating system in it, so she warmed up. She was looking everywhere as they drove home. She was excited to see so many white people. When they got to her brother's house, she discovered that he lived in a white dominated area in Hampstead. His wife welcomed Uzonna, and the children all came out to see me. After the welcome, she was shown her room, where she put her little bag. She was told to freshen up and then come downstairs.

When she came downstairs, the first thing her brother told me was, 'If my wife says that you can stay with us, then you will do so. But at any time if she decides that you can no longer stay with us, I will make sure I sent you home.' She just looked at him and shook her head in response.

Then his wife said that tomorrow the children would be going to school and would need to be ready by 7.30 a.m. She told her what they would need, what they would eat, what time to wake them up, where their school uniforms were kept, what to pack in their lunch bags, where their shoes were kept, and who had baths in the morning. That was Uzonna's first lesson. The next lesson was to learn what food the children liked, how to cook it, when to prepare the food, and how to serve it. She also learned what drinks they liked with their food, what utensils they used, what corner of the table each one of them sat at, what time she should wake them in the mornings, and what cereal each one of them liked. Uzonna was told that the most important part of her duties was to make sure the children were happy and well cared for. That was not going to be hard for her, because she naturally loved children and her brother, and she would do everything she could to make the children happy.

It did not take her very long to earn the love and the trust of the children. She usually read bedtime stories to the children, and while reading she made some noises and movements that they liked, especially the youngest son. Sometimes when she was very busy with housework and cooking for the family, the mother would offer to read to them, but they would refuse. The youngest would start to cry, saying that he only wanted Uzonna to read to him, because his mother would not be able to animate the stories. She had a wonderful relationship with the children, and they felt happy and safe with her. They taught her a lot of things about England and tried so hard to help her with English pronunciations.

The children were not what made her life hard, but the other part of the whole affairs within the house. She had to do all cooking for the family and clean the house (which had four flats each of three bedroom), and it must be proper cleaning because the master of the house never liked to see any mark on the floors. Anytime he saw a mark in the house, he would call Uzonna to come and remove the mark. It was a constant duty because the children could not stop playing in the house, using their shoes to make black marks on the floor. Life became a bit unhappy; there were no friends to visit, and even if she had friends, there would be no time to visit them. She used to stand by the window in her room when she had nothing to do, looking out and watching the people that were walking past the house. It was a very lonely and miserable period for Uzonna. She was used to having people around all the time before coming to London. The children used to keep her company, but not all the time because they too had their friends and homework to attend to. Moreover, their companionship was very different from that of the children from home, who spoke the same language and could play the same way as Uzonna did. It felt like she was under house arrest. She did not know anywhere or anybody—her life was just cooking, looking after the children, and doing all the washing by hand (because she did not know how to use the washing machine).

It was not all miserable, because due to the type of the job the master of the house had, she had the opportunity to meet some of the very important dignitaries from countries around the world. She had the chance to prepare dinner for prime ministers like Arnold Smith, James Callaghan; for many African leaders like General Gown of Nigeria and General Obasanjo; and some ambassadors and diplomats from many countries like Australia and New Zealand. In doing so, sometimes she could not go to bed until around 2.00 a.m., or even later than that, but that did not bother her so much.

The problem she had for the first few weeks was the fact that her nephews said that they did not understand what she said to them due to her accent. Whenever she spoke to them, they became angry and would start to laugh at her. This made her very sad, but she did not know how to change her accent because she was not interacting with other people. One day the children complained again to their parents, who then said that they were going to send Uzonna to college to learn how to speak proper English. The mother took her to college the next day to register for learning English as a foreign language. After registration, Uzonna's sister-in-law paid the appropriate college fees, and she was told to start the following week. On the way back to the house, Uzonna was told that she was only going to college to learn how to speak proper English, and not to make friends. She must not stay back to chat with the other students after lessons, because they would only mislead her, and she must remember that she was in a foreign land.

As agreed with the college, Uzonna started college the following week. It was an eye-opener, and even though she was warned not to make friends, she did make some. The students were very helpful and considerate. The lessons helped a lot, and within a period of three months her English-speaking ability improved so much that the children could understand her very well, they stopped complaining to their parents, and her relationship with the family improved. The children started to ask her to read to them during bedtime.

After three months of being at home, cooking and doing all the housework, it was time for Uzonna to start proper college so as to build a career for the future. She wanted to do nursing, but that was turned down by the madam of the house, who said that going into nursing would defeat the purpose of them spending all that money to bring Uzonna to the United Kingdom. She said that Uzonna going into nursing would make her move into the hospital hostel, and there would be no one to look after the children, which was the main reason they brought her to London. Uzonna had no knowledge that if she had gone into nursing school, she would have been allowed to stay in London, so she went along with what the madam and her husband decided. They found a college for her, and she registered to start secretarial studies.

Every morning during the school term, Uzonna would have to wake up around five in the morning, use the bathroom, and get the children up one by one. She got them ready by making them use the bathroom, giving them their school uniforms, and dressing them. They then went downstairs, and Uzonna would ask them what they wanted for breakfast; each one would demand different things. She would prepare whatever breakfast they wanted, set them on the table for them, and sit with them to make sure they ate. After they had their breakfast, Uzonna would then clear the table, wash up, and bring their school bags down for them so that their mother could drive them to school.

Uzonna would then rush upstairs to get ready to go to college with very little time. She never had time to have breakfast, so most mornings she would just grab a loaf of bread, put it into her bag, and run down to the tube station.

One morning as she was about to run down the staircase to the train platform, she heard the gate inspector say to her, 'Why can you not ever woke up early enough to have time to get ready for college, so that you can stop running down all the time?'

Uzonna said to herself, I wish this lady knew the time I woke every morning, and the amount of work I have to do before leaving the house to go to college. When she got to the college, she would then eat half of the loaf for breakfast and drink water from the tap; the other half would be for lunch.

Going to college made lots of changes to Uzonna's life. She met lots of good people within the college, and the teachers were wonderfully kind and caring. The students were very accommodating, friendly, helpful, and supportive. It made her realise that there were people out there who prepared to help anyone who needed help, no matter from where they came. The first three months at the college were a great learning period. Students from top families extended hands of friendship to me. She learnt later that some of their parents were medical doctors or top government officials. Many of them became very good friends with Uzonna, and some even offered her some of their lunches. They asked her to go to the canteen with them, but she told them that she had no money to buy any food. They kept asking her why she had always had bread in the morning and during lunch as well. 'Don't you get fed up eating bread every day?' To them it was not nice, but to Uzonna it was a luxury, coming from that type of background. She only had bread when those who visited my auntie brought some for her. Her auntie never gave her bread. Whenever she had bread with her children or on her own, she cut the crust and put it into the dirty water she used to wash her hand. She would gave Uzonna two pence to use to buy breakfast for the morning because she felt Uzonna was not good enough to eat bread with her children. Uzonna would then buy one penny of akara and one penny of agidi. She believed that even if Uzonna's father was still alive, he would not had been able to buy bread for everyone, so she had to keep me as a very poor man's daughter, and eating bread in her house would mean that Uzonna would be like her children.

Eating bread morning and afternoon was nothing to Uzonna. She felt she was making up for the past years of not being able to eat bread. She did not feel the need to explain all that to the girls, because they would not have understood where she was coming from. She just started crying—there were so much emotions flowing out. Uzonna had never had anyone care for her like the girls. She was overcome by emotion to see how people of different races cared for her. She had never experienced care or love from anyone; she had always been disliked and treated as slave who had no emotions and did not get tired working. She was not good enough to have decent clothes and shoes, and she was not someone who would always be spoken to without respect. In fact to see that the students found her to be a human being made her feel very emotional.

She had a wonderful time at college. She also found out that she was not as bad as it was made out while she was in Nigeria. Uzonna was doing very well in her studies. While she was in Nigeria, she was made to believe that she could never pass any of her examinations—she was only to be a house girl, which was why she was brought to England. She put every effort into her studies because she wanted to prove to people that if she was given a good chance, good support, and a good studying environment, she could do better. Uzonna was able to pass her typing stage three, her shorthand with a hundred words per minute, commerce, English O-level, office practice, and other subjects, giving her a good diploma in secretarial studies.

She was very pleased with herself, but that did not impress her family because some of them had studied at Cambridge and Oxford, and those that went to university in Nigeria attended very highly rated universities. But for Uzonna it was the beginning of a bright future, and this led her into gaining higher qualifications, thereby building up her self-confidence.

During her time at college, she learnt that individuals had rights to be respected and to be treated as human, not like animals. Her eyes were opened at college about some of the things she did not know, like contraceptives. She found that every English girl knew of it. Some of the students told her to go to her doctor and find out more about it.

As time went on, Uzonna was allowed to spend some time at college after lessons doing her assignments, because the children did not need to have their supper until six o'clock. She could get home around five o'clock and still have enough time to prepare the food, make sure they had their baths, change them into their pyjamas, and get them ready to go to bed at eight.

One day at college, one of her friends fell ill and needed someone to take her home. Uzonna said she was going to take her home as long as the girl told her how to get back to Victoria Station, because she would find her way home from there. Uzonna went to the house with her friend, made sure she was all right, and made some quick pepper soup for her. Then she asked her how to get to Victoria. The friend told her to go to the train station and take a train. Uzonna thought she meant any train that came to that station, so she got onto the first train that arrived at the platform, not knowing that the train was destined to travel to Glasgow without stopping at Victoria.

Uzonna became worried because it was getting late, and she did not tell her madam that she was going anywhere after college. She started sweating and panicking, and she walked to the apartment where the train guard was standing, asking him when the train would get to Victoria. He said, 'Which Victoria?'

'The one in London.'

He then told her that the train was very far away from London and was heading to Glasgow. When he saw the fear in her eyes, he asked her where she was going. Uzonna told him she was trying to go home, which was very close to Chalk Farm station. He asked her where she came from, and how long she had been in England. She admitted it was not very long. He told her to stay with him and said he would put her into another train, going back to London; he would tell the train to put down at Victoria Station. When the train stopped at a station, the guard took her across the platform and handed her over to another train guard, who was standing on the platform. He asked him to put her onto a train going to Victoria and make sure she got off at the right station.

In the end Uzonna got on the right way going home, but it was already very dark, and the people she was living with had already reported her missing to the police. As she got to Victoria Station, she was met by the police, who then asked her what had happened. She told them her story, and they took her home and told her to always ask the train guards whenever she was not sure where the trains were going. It was very reassuring to know that people and police were very kind and helpful.

College was nice, and in the end after she got her diploma, Uzonna had offers of jobs, but she ended up working with NatWest Bank. It was great going from being a house girl to being a bank employee—what a big difference!

It was during the time Uzonna was working with the bank that she met a young man. She later married him after going out with him for two years. Though they went out for two years, at first she was only allowed to see him once a month for two hours—and that did not give her enough time to find out that he drank a lot. She did not realise that marrying him would be putting her into a big fire, but there were some positive things that came out of the marriage. She was blessed with two glorious sons who really went through a lot of difficult times with her due to their father's drinking problem. It was very difficult raising them, but God was merciful to them.

Uzonna worked with very respectable people in the bank and enjoyed the job. After some years with the bank, she had to give up the job due to her childcare being unreliable, but she had to find another job quickly because she had to feed and clothe the children, and then pay for their day care. She was lucky to get a job with St Luke's Therapeutic Unit, a home for highly emotionally disturbed children. During her interview, she was asked why she left the bank, and she told them her problem with finding a good babysitter. The director of the unit was very kind, and she said Uzonna could bring the children to the home after school; they could stay with the other children in the sitting room, watching television, playing games, or reading until Uzonna finished work for the day. All she needed was someone to take them to school, and the director even allowed her to take the unit's car to take them to school, pick them after school, and then bring them to the unit. In other to do so, she had to change her lunch time to three o'clock in the afternoon, to enable her to pick them up, but she was very happy to do so.

Working with St. Lukes Therapeutic Unit was very rewarding to Uzonna. It helped her to bring out all the emotions within her which she had never had the opportunity to express. She could work with the children very well and understand their predicaments—the rejection, the abuse, the neglect, starvation, the fear of being alive, always wishing that they were better off dead. She felt like one of them, and their situations reminded her a lot of her past life. The fact that she had a very kind and understanding boss helped her to work out her emotions and then move ahead.

On one of the meetings with parents, one couple said that they were ready to take their son home with them. It was great news for the staff and the boy. He had been wishing and praying that his mother and stepfather would take him home. He loved his mother very much. He was taken to the shop by staff to buy clothes, shoes, and all the necessary things he needed. All the children and staff in the home bought a farewell card, signed it, and contributed some money to put into the card. They waited to give it to him on the final day. On the given date, his parents arrived and went into the director's office, and the staff brought out the boy's suitcase, put it by the doorway, gave the card signed by all the children and staff within the home with all the money collected, and said good-bye to him. When the parents came out of the office, Uzonna and the staff asked them if they could put their son's belongings into their car.

His mother said no—her partner had threatened to kick her out of her house if her son came home with them. He said that he could not stand any child to come between them. It was very devastating, and the director did not know how to tell the boy what had transpired.

The couple left the building without the boy. He thought that they had gone to get something and were coming back to pick him up. We could not even try to take his suitcase back to the room—everything was left by the door because they were waiting after the director had spoken to him. The staff was prepared for his tantrum, and then the director called the boy into her office, as well as two staff she knew the boy liked and respected. They told the boy what the parents had said. He threw himself on the floor and started screaming, saying that he was going to kill himself. He said his mother did not love him. The boy cried uncontrollably, and Uzonna joined him. She was unable to eat or do much that day; the rejection of the boy by his mother made the boy feel that he was not loved at all by his mother and by people around him. It really brought out her own feelings of never being loved or cared for by anybody. It was a very painful day. After a while the boy stopped crying, and many of the staff and the other children within the home comforted him, but Uzonna carried on crying.

The boss took her into her office and said that she was sure that the boy's incident did affect me, but she felt that there was more to it. Uzonna told her most of her life story. The director said that she now knew why Uzonna did her job with the children in the unit very well; she noticed that Uzonna took good care of them. Uzonna was very much emotionally attached to the children and always found it very difficult to bear seeing children suffer. Working at St Luke's Unit played a great part in her life; it was like having sessions with counsellors, because it gave her the opportunity to resolve some of the painful issues she had in her life. The unit was like a large family, where all the staff were brothers and sisters, while the children at the home as the group's children. Such a working environment would never exist now; things changed a lot since the 1970s and 1980s.

It was a big blow that, after a year and some months working at St Luke's, they received the sad news that the unit would be closed, because the government could no longer afford to keep it open. With help from Social Services and other organizations, the children in the unit were placed into other units in different parts of the country; some were placed back with their natural parents, and some were put into foster homes. After all the children were finally placed in safe homes, the unit closed, and all the staff lost their jobs.

Then another phase of Uzonna's life began. The school where her sons attended wrote to her to tell her that her second son would no longer be accommodated in the school, because the school could not control his hyperactive behaviour. The school recommended that she take him to a special school, because he was only four and a half years old. Uzonna tried getting him into another school, but to no avail. There was always the question of why he did not go to the same school with his brother. In the end she was not able to find him another school. She then spoke to her older sister, who was at the time living in Boston. Her sister's advice to Uzonna was to take him back home to Nigeria. Uzonna had no parents, so who was she going to send her son to? In the end she made up my mind to go back to Nigeria with the boys, hoping to get some help from the extended family.

The stay in Nigeria was full of suffering. The sons were very physically, emotionally, and mentally abused. For Uzonna, it was also hell. The comments the sons made on their return to the UK said it all. As soon as the plane touched down at Heathrow Airport, they said, 'Mum, we are now out of prison.' When she told them that she had no money to buy food or clothes for them, they said it was better for them to starve than be at home with their father.

They were now back in the United Kingdom with nothing, no money or food, but things did not get bad as they had envisaged. There was a very good-hearted family who stood by them, providing them with food and bedding. The family looked after one of Uzonna's sons like their own child. There were no words to express Uzonna's gratitude to them for their kindness, and the fact that they stood by the family during their most difficult time. Uzonna prayed, May the Good Lord continue to bless them, guide them, and always be by their side.

The difficult experience the boys had while they were in Nigeria helped them a lot in being able to cope with difficult situations they came across in university. They learnt that one needed a good education to get a good job, and they also found out that being an alcoholic would definitely destroy their lives, so they kept away from it.

Life within the UK was not a bed of roses; things were very tough, including getting education, jobs, and good accommodations, but one could not compare it to what the family went through in Nigeria. Life was a big struggle, but Uzonna refused to let the struggle pull her down. It was the lifestyle here: one had to struggle to survive in whatever part of the world one lived.

The experiences Uzonna had while growing up had great influence in her life. She was always strong in difficult situations and could bear suffering more than most of her friends. Things that most people took to be very difficult would appear mild to her. People got easily heartbroken over little things, but Uzonna found them to be normal. Sometimes people thought that she was not a normal woman, saying that she had a different mind. They found her very strong-hearted.

Lightning Source UK Ltd.
Milton Keynes UK
UKOW040937130712

195912UK00001B/20/P